for the love of

Simple Linework

- a diary of an artist -

arvind narale

Text Edited by

Dr. Ratnakar Narale
Toronto, Ontario

Published by

Canadian Stage & Arts Publications Ltd.
1100 Caledonia Road
Toronto, Ontario
M6A 2W5
Phone : (416) 785 4311

Produced by

Creative Group 2
Toronto, Ontario

... *for the love of*

Simple Linework

ISBN 0-919952-37-2
Toronto, 1994
Printed in Canada

Copyright ©1994
Creative Group 2, Toronto

● English Edition

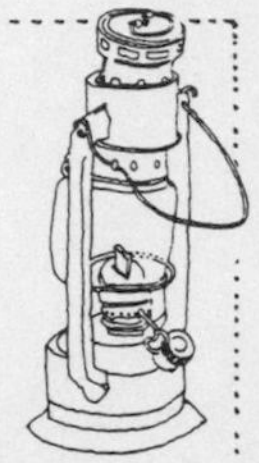

Let me trod the humble path,
Leading to countryside;
Converse in the local tongue,
To friends, bona fide !

THE COVER : On-site study of the bas-relief in stone, at the Great Temple of Amun, Karnak, during the author's cruise through the Nile.

Acknowledgements

The author would like to extend the heartfelt thanks to Mr. Waghe, his primary school teacher, who introduced him to the magic of simple line-drawing during the childhood days. Also, he would like to acknowledge the valuable guidance he received from his instructor Mr. Deshpande, during the intermediate school years.

The author also would like to express his earnest gratitude to Mr. Brian Brooks, who exposed him to the beauty of freehand *linework*.

Lines link the unlinked,
And unlink the links;
The ink links the things,
That no one possibly thinks !

Preface

I was about five years of age then. In a small town in India, my teacher, Mr. Waghe, used to give me lessons in mathematics and arts. Mr. Waghe was very gentle by nature. He took great pleasure in teaching children and was adored by all his pupils. At the end of the lesson, whether it was mathematics or art, he liked to draw funny little sketches of animals and birds, to end the class on a happy note. He drew them with such an ease and in so few lines that, to me, it was an astonishing feat.

Thirty years later, I started working in one of the bigger architectural offices in Toronto. Here again, the drawings of my supervisor, Mr. Brian Brooks, caught my eye. As an architect, I always liked line-drawings. However, the way Mr. Brooks drew the lines, or rather, as the lines came out of his pen, they appeared so meaningful and special that, to me, they were hypnotizing !

Both the *gurus* seemed to have one attribute in common. They were quite natural in their approach of drawing lines. I always wondered if I could develop this art for myself. Therefore, I often quietly studied Mr. Brooks' architectural sketches, mostly drawn on tracing paper. Literally copying his technique and experimenting with it over a long period, I discovered that in order to produce a line of good quality, one must concentrate and focus on the line as it unfolds. It is only then - after developing a sensitivity to the emerging product - that the *linework* assumes a unique quality of its own.

Here, an attempt has been made to share my experience with others, so that those interested in learning this art, also could enjoy the magical beauty hidden in simple *linework*. It is my sincere desire that the effort of compiling the following material will be beneficial to them.

Welcome to the world of lines. Enjoy the sensitivity of the freehand lines as they assume different shapes, forms and characteristics.

Arvind Narale

A tribute to my revered teachers

The author has fond memories of the Indian village life, the vegetation and the animal life around. Also, he feels deeply indebted to and closely connected with his art teachers, who introduced him to the wonderful world of drawing.

Is there a man, who, on the earth begotten,
Has his motherland completely forgotten ?
And, yet thinks, becoming a grown-up man,
Be possible, without his childhood, can !

Or, put it this way . . .
Could the enlarging circular ripples,
In still-waters, be so vain;
As to forget - their existence,
Originated with a drop of rain ?

Or, this way . . .
Higher and higher, climbing a kite,
Touching the clouds and the skies,
Breathing fresh air, the new atmosphere,
Looks back to earth with each rise;
Can the kite ignore its connection,
Considering it past, and far at ground ?
Puffing with pride, daring break the tie,
It wouldn't be any more around !

Or, simply this way . . .
Ocean has the biggest heart, all drops to contain,
Many rise up, change to clouds, large heights to attain;
Forget they not, the origin - their special privilege;
Shed tears, by shower of rains, thus paying homage !

Therefore . . .
Uniqueness, truly I find, and also a strange mystery;
In the reference, the reverence, and the joy of past history !

Dedicated
to
Annaji
Akka
Saral
and
Vimal

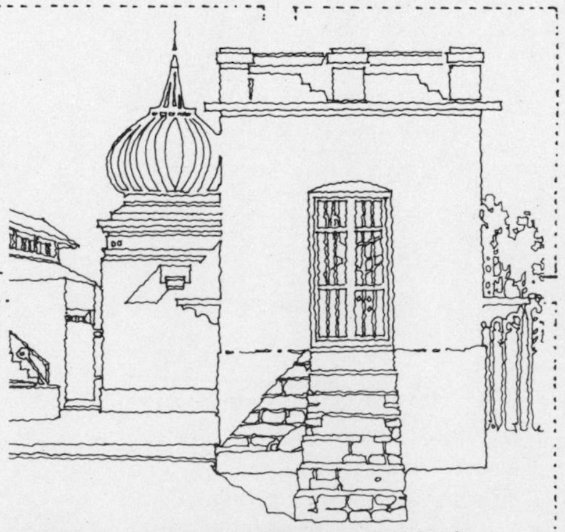

Temple of Hanuman and Goddess Durga, Katol, India

Contents

The main tool used for the sketches in this book is a *Rapid-o-graph* pen. The tool employed, produces different results depending on the technique of implementation. The style that forms the fabric of the present work is my personal fascination. Of course, every individual may develop his own style.

In the present work, I have approached the subject in logically arranged stages. At the outset I have discussed the basic tools employed for producing a *linework*. Then I have explained how I had developed a habit of occupying my mind with the activity of drawing quick little sketches. Seemingly an unimportant start, but in reality it is the foundation for developing a creative perception. Further, I have covered the important fundamentals; such as, the *basic form, scale and proportions*, etc., for step by step build up of a sketch.

I have then examined various ideas and techniques utilized in drawing sketches and elucidated them in detail with suitable examples.

The present work is especially designed to make it useful for the students of art, of all age groups, at all times, and literally in any part of the world. The work should prove itself valuable for amateurs and the professionals, alike.

It is my sincere desire that the disclosure of my experience, related to drawing the sketches with freehand lines, will inspire you, too, to discover the magical beauty hidden in simple *linework*!

Author

Introduction
... in a nutshell

Amazing is the magic of freehand lines !

Freehand *linework* is perhaps the most elementary medium, that could be employed by anyone to acquire the basic skill of drawing. And yet, if developed properly, it could open up the world of creating attractive sketches having beauty with simplicity. Indeed, with practice, once the skill is acquired, it would become natural for you to add a unique touch to your sketches.

CHAPTER ONE

The medium and the tools
... the equipment

A freehand line drawn with a *Rapid-o-graph* pen, is the basic medium explored in the present work. An approach of sketching with ink lines is commonly known as the *pen & ink* technique. In this method, the use of shading - a gradual change of tone - is completely absent.

Instead of a *Rapid-o-graph*, a felt tipped pen or a pencil also can be used, similarly. The comparative features of these three tools are explained in this chapter.

● Pencil

a.　A pencil produces uneven lines unless its tip is kept sharp constantly, which may not be practical. The lead loses its point quickly, more so, on a coarse paper.

b.　A hard pencil maintains its point, but does not produce a dark black line. A soft pencil offers darkness, but its tip wares out quickly.

c.　The advantage of using a pencil is that mistakes can be easily erased.

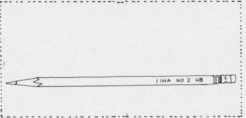

↑
Notice the softness of a pencil-line in the adjoining sketch. The uneven lines have resulted into a textured effect. However, this quality could be used as an advantage, where the uniformity of lines is not important.

● Felt tipped pen

a.　It yields a uniform line, until its tip loses the sharpness.

b.　It produces a relatively less black line than the *Indian Ink* used in a *Rapid-o-graph*.

c.　A uniform gradation of tips is not available to cover a wide range of line thicknesses.

d.　It is significantly less expensive than a *Rapid-o-graph*.

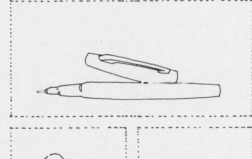

↑
Notice the softness of the lines. They are not as uniform as the lines drawn by a *Rapid-o-graph*, as is evident in the next sketch.

In a sketch, where a sudden change in the thickness, within a line, is required, a felt tipped pen is more suitable than a *Rapid-o-graph*.

● Rapid-o-graph

a.　It produces a uniform line, throughout the length.

b.　The *Indian Ink* used in it, produces a solid black line.

c.　A wider range of nib sizes is available to draw lines of various thicknesses.

d.　Although comparatively more expensive, its durability justifies the cost.

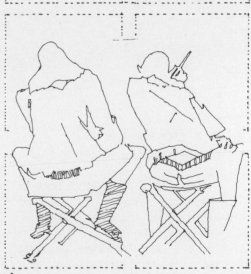

↑
The lines are crisp. They are uniform in darkness throughout the sketch. Their width is rigidly confined and, therefore, they look committed, as compared to the lines drawn with the other two tools.

CHAPTER TWO

Quick little sketches

. . . the right beginning

When I was a little boy in grade one, our teacher, Mr. Waghe, introduced us to the art of creating fascinating pictures with simple lines. On the first day, he drew a single freehand line and showed us how easily it could be developed into a sketch of an object.

From each line, he would develop a different object for each student. And then, in turn he would ask each of us to draw another object using a similar straight line.

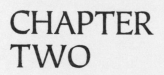

We found this exercise very amusing. I was eager to discover as many objects as possible that could be formed the same way. At once it became a challenge to my mind.

Looking back, I remember, I was obsessed by the idea of looking for objects that could be drawn with simple straight lines. My way of observing things was thus steered in this particular direction. Though, now, this exercise feels childish, it was the trigger behind a creative thinking, required to cultivate a mind.

For the next step, he drew a pair of lines and showed us, how it also can be developed into a number of different objects.

Again, the challenge was to discover and draw as many such objects as possible.

I disclosed these ideas to my other friends. Soon, the children in the neighbourhood caught the excitement of searching for newer objects. It became our common pastime for a considerable period..

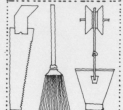

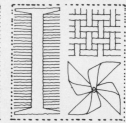

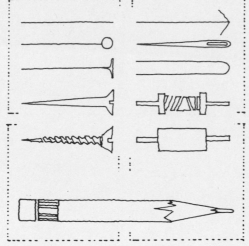

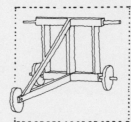

As more details are shown, the picture unfolds itself. An object, such as a comb, is made up of a number of repetitive lines, a quality that gives the object an interesting texture.

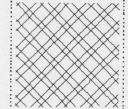

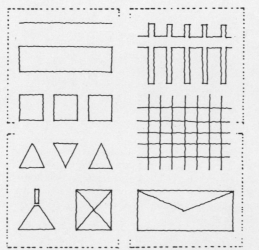

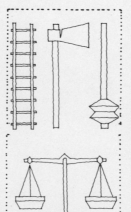

Notice, how easy it is to draw the familiar objects, using straight lines. Sometimes, a sketch, such as that of a pencil or a hanger, can be drawn with two or three lines only. In many cases, once the major *linework* is properly shown, it is easy to fill the details.

With a bit of practice, it becomes easier to tackle the objects seemingly difficult to draw. An intricate sketch of a cobweb is easy to translate on paper, once its repetitive pattern is understood.

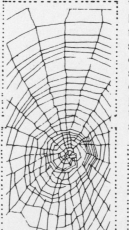

Mr. Waghe was very innovative. He knew how to keep the enthusiasm afresh among his students. In the subsequent lessons, he asked us to draw several pictures of an object to form a group. We drew such groups, taking a new object each time.

← Even a group of just two elements looks better than a single item. In a larger group there certainly exists a relationship among its elements, which adds interest to the sketch.

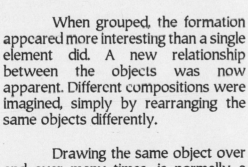

When grouped, the formation appeared more interesting than a single element did. A new relationship between the objects was now apparent. Different compositions were imagined, simply by rearranging the same objects differently.

Drawing the same object over and over many times, is normally a monotonous exercise, and therefore, students do not enjoy it. However, through this new idea our teacher induced us to do the same, but with fun.

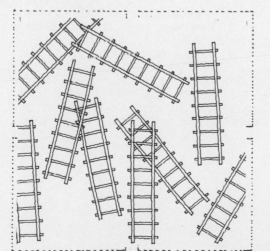

Next followed the magic of a curved line. The idea opened up the treasure of drawing practically every object, with lines - straight and curved. It was easy too ! Looking back, I remember, I must have drawn hundreds of such quick little sketches.

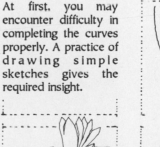

At first, you may encounter difficulty in completing the curves properly. A practice of drawing simple sketches gives the required insight.

The objects, like light bulbs or mangos, can be drawn with one continuous curved line, without much detail added to them. To sum up an object in a nut-shell, that is all you need to draw.

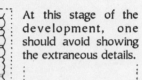

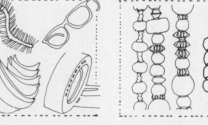

At this stage of the development, one should avoid showing the extraneous details.

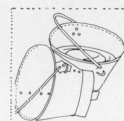

The sketches of most of the objects we see around, can be drawn as a combination of curved and straight lines. Draw as many objects as you can, to build up a confidence.

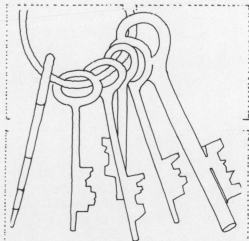

In the beginning, I felt comfortable drawing the sketches in very small size in order to keep the mistakes inconspicuous.

When a sketch was drawn to a large size, naturally the mistakes became obvious. At this stage of learning, I wanted to enjoy the fun of drawing, more than its correctness.

Though the village life did not offer modern objects to draw, certainly there was ample local material available for practice.

After a sufficient practice, I was amused to see my own progress. I wanted to experiment drawing numerous objects, from little bugs to big elephants. Regardless of their size, the process of drawing itself put my imagination to test.

Gradually, I ventured to draw them bigger and bigger in size, to find my own mistakes.

Some objects were easy to tackle. Some were challenging. Some were simply funny. But, all of them had their own charm.

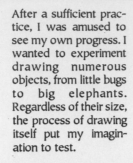

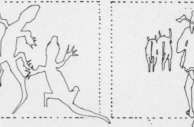

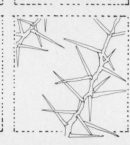

At times, I did not like my own sketches, since they looked inept. I was still happy because I relished the sheer process of drawing and the fun of even just looking at the failures!

 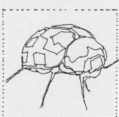 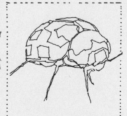

Gradually, we ventured to experiment with larger sketches, even when we knew that the mistakes would be magnified.

In spite of our failures, our teacher encouraged us to draw more and more. It helped us build confidence and keep our tempo up. This made us adore him and take him as a good friend.

Soon, the habit of making quick little sketches took me over. Fortunately, in the vicinity, there never was a scarcity of objects to draw. And, I desired to sketch almost everything that I saw around.

I drew the sketches in pencil, and I enjoyed it at every step.

Use of a soft pencil enabled me to erase the mistakes easily. It was the only tool available, those days.

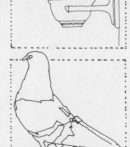

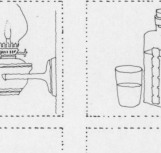

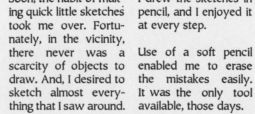 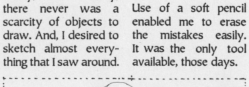

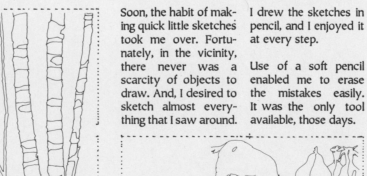 

The teacher lent us all, his very mind,
And showed the limit of being kind;
Allowed us to enter, through his art,
The gateway of his precious heart!

CHAPTER THREE

Basic forms

... visualizing the overall shapes.

I was in grade seven now. The habit of drawing sketches, very basic in nature, was still active in me. I was constantly struggling to draw objects to their exactness, but often without success. I could not quite understand what was going wrong.

At this juncture, my intermediate school teacher, Mr. Deshpande, a devout art instructor, noticed the dilemma. He cautioned me not to aim for exactness at the outset, without knowing certain fundamentals first. He suggested that, to achieve exactness, I must grasp two basal but important steps. First, learn to visualize the *basic form* of the object. Secondly, study the object in relation to its correct *scale and proportions*.

The *basic form* of any object is its simplified overall shape. In a more complex object, the *basic form* is the summation of the individual forms of its elements.

The way of looking at an object, as made of straight and curved lines, had to be developed into an approach of finding its *basic form*. I was then convinced that any object, animate or inanimate, could be summed up into its *basic form*. And that, the finished sketch is merely an elaboration of its *basic form*, developed further by modifying the profile and adding the required details.

A common tendency of adding too many lines, in an attempt to beautify the sketch or to cover up the mistakes, exists in the beginning with many students of art. I was no exception. And, it did not escape the keen eye of our instructor. He insisted on utilizing the least amount of *linework*, conveying its fullest meaning. The key to simple sketching was thus acquired.

To develop a good hand, one must practise a lot. The ability to visualize the *basic forms*, is truly the key to encounter the situations, simple or complex. The superfluous part of a *linework* does not add to the quality of the sketch. Rather, it subtracts. I find, the least is the best.

The process of drawing a *basic form* of simple objects is as follows :

Step 1

Draw with straight or curved lines, an overall shape of the body of the object. Usually the body, up to the neck line, occupies the largest area.

Step 2

Add shapes of other individual elements to the body, as shown in figures below. It sums up the *basic form* of an object.

Step 3

Using these *basic forms* as guidelines, work out proper profiles of the components carefully.

Step 4

Add only the necessary details. Erase the construction lines carefully. The sketch of an object is now ready, using a minimum *linework*.

● A proper sequence
of drawing the *basic form* of a more complex object :

Assume that you are drawing one of the following objects placed in front of you :

A GIRL PLAYING MUSIC
A BUNCH OF CORN EARS
AN ANIMAL SITTING ON A BRANCH

Use of a pencil is recommended for this part of the exercise. For, an incorrect profile can be easily rectified with the help of an eraser.

Step 1

Contemplate on the object to be drawn. Analyze in your mind, the overall shape of the object, including the adjoining elements, if any. This can be done by looking at the object with squinted eyes. By doing so, you will see the profile of the object more clearly than the details.

The first diagram, in each case, shows the grey polygon, just large enough to encompass the object completely.

Step 2

The figures in column 1 on page 8, show two approaches of developing the *basic form*, conceptually.

The first approach is to build the form with straight lines within the polygon, as shown in the cases of A GIRL PLAYING MUSIC, and A BUNCH OF CORN EARS. This approach further involves carving out from the polygon, the areas that do not form the part of the object.

The second approach is to build the form with curved lines, as shown in the case of AN ANIMAL SITTING ON A BRANCH. This approach suggests building up of the figure with curved shapes, in their conceptual form.

Use either of the two methods, to complete the external profile of the object to your satisfaction.

Step 3

Carve out the internal areas that do not form the part of the sketch. Then subdivide the area of the sketch into major segments to identify the major parts, by drawing their shapes as shown by the dotted lines.

In the case of A GIRL PLAYING MUSIC, the major parts are the head, dress, hands and musical instrument. It is a good practice to construct the larger segments first, followed by the smaller ones.

You may not be able to draw the correct shapes of these segments in the first attempt. Keep correcting, until you are convinced that the directional tilt and the interrelationship of segments are correctly shown.

Now, subdivide these major segments into a number of subsegments, to represent the individual elements.

In the case of A GIRL PLAYING MUSIC, the individual elements are - the areas of head cover, the face, the hair, the shirt sleeves, the shirt, the hands, the skirt and the musical instrument.

In the sketch of AN ANIMAL SITTING ON A BRANCH, the subdivisions are made by corresponding curved shapes.

The development of the actual drawing from the *basic form* in Step 3, is graphically illustrated in the Steps 4, 5 & 6.

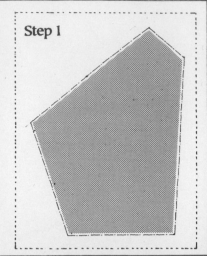

Step 1 On the left is shown A GIRL PLAYING MUSIC.

→

Step 2 On the right, is shown the corresponding polygon that snugly covers the area of the object. The shaded part is the maximum area, within which the object is to be drawn. No part of the drawing projects beyond this area.

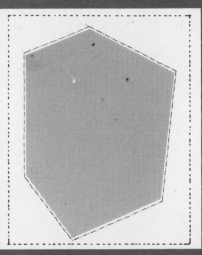

Step 1 On the left is shown A BUNCH OF CORN EARS.

→

Step 2 On the right, is shown the corresponding polygon that snugly covers the area of the object. The shaded part is the maximum area, within which the object is to be drawn. No part of the drawing projects beyond this area.

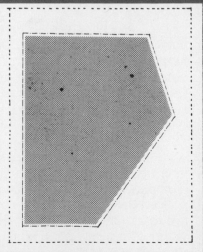

Step 1 On the left is shown the sketch of AN ANIMAL SITTING ON A BRANCH.

→

Step 2 On the right, is shown the corresponding polygon that snugly covers the area of the object. For an object with a rounded profile, the use of curved lines, as against the straight edges, is more suitable to construct its *basic form*.

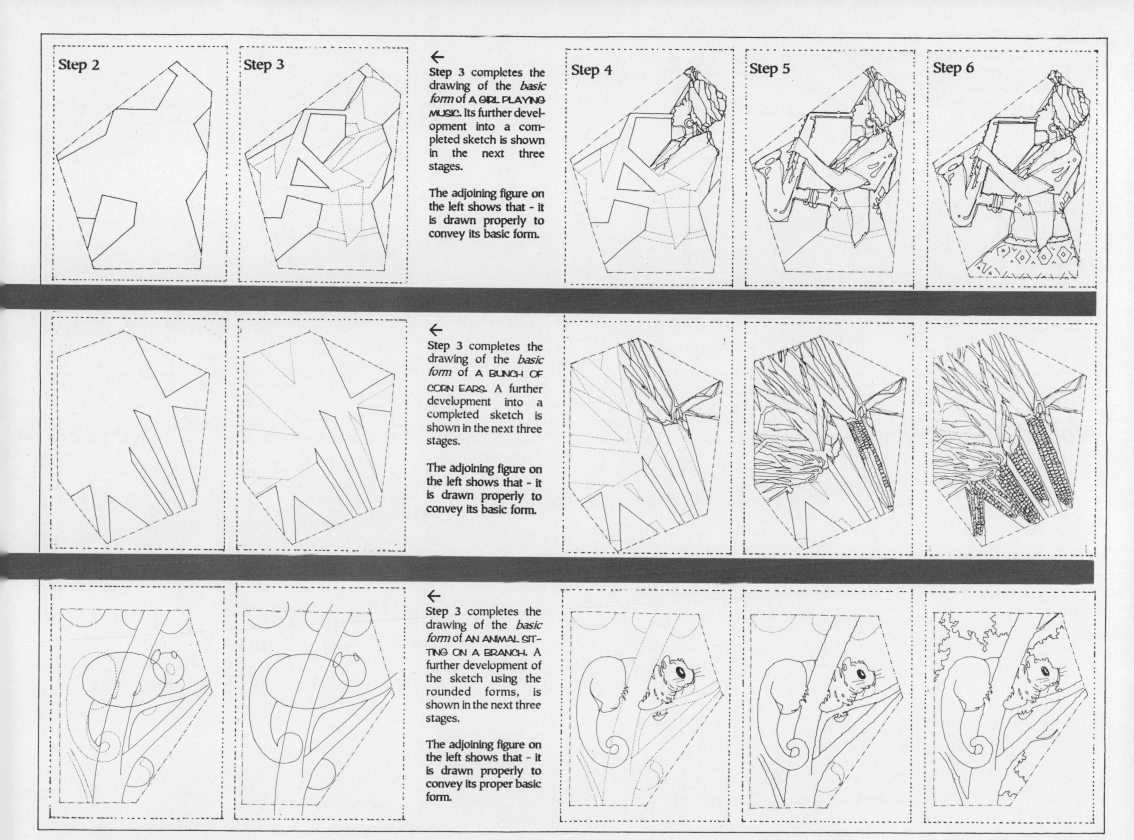

Step 2

Step 3

← Step 3 completes the drawing of the *basic form* of A GIRL PLAYING MUSIC. Its further development into a completed sketch is shown in the next three stages.

The adjoining figure on the left shows that - it is drawn properly to convey its basic form.

Step 4

Step 5

Step 6

← Step 3 completes the drawing of the *basic form* of A BUNCH OF CORN EARS. A further development into a completed sketch is shown in the next three stages.

The adjoining figure on the left shows that - it is drawn properly to convey its basic form.

← Step 3 completes the drawing of the *basic form* of AN ANIMAL SITTING ON A BRANCH. A further development of the sketch using the rounded forms, is shown in the next three stages.

The adjoining figure on the left shows that - it is drawn properly to convey its proper basic form.

In my tiny village in India, the presence of different animals and colourful vegetation around, was a common sight. It provided me with a plenty of material to practice with. Only, I had to put my mind and heart into it, remembering the above points.

About this time, noticing my keen interest in drawing, our teacher presented me with a diary. As per his advice, I carried it with me all the time to draw sketches of all types. I drew lots and lots of sketches, wherever I went.

AT HOME

I tried to sketch most of the activities occurring on a daily basis. At home I could take my own time to draw them. Everyone encouraged me in this activity.

A colourful cock crowed in the morn,
The natural sign of a village alarm;
Elderly, then, to the youth warn,
To get up and prepare for the farm.

The cock having done its duty,
Started for its stomach's search;
Twice observed its own beauty,
Before the family behind it march.

A colourful ROOSTER AND ITS FAMILY were a common sight. The family roamed all over, wandering aimlessly, perhaps trying to stay away from the humans.

←
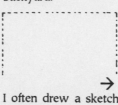

THE BRIGHT RED POMEGRANATES were relished by the children and the birds alike. The fruit, packed with juicy seeds, hung in clusters on the trees in our backyard.

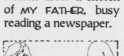
→
I often drew a sketch of MY FATHER, busy reading a newspaper.

←

←
A colourful ROOSTER AND ITS FAMILY were a common sight.

The sight of THE ENTRANCE GATE of our compound wall, with the temple in the background, always fascinated me.

IN THE GARDEN

A visit to the nearby gardens offered an ample opportunity to draw sketches of all types of vegetation, fruits, flowers and the animals around.

Grass looked greener, on the other side of the fence,
Neighbour's flowers looked, colourful and dense;
Occasionally plucked one, from their garden,
To apologize later, "I beg your pardon !"

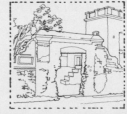
↑
The garden of our house, though small, had a number of DENSE FRUIT TREES in it. Different colourful flowers and variety of vegetation added a charm to it. I sketched most of it.

→
THE MONKEYS appeared conspicuous with their reddish face. These monkeys jumped from tree to tree, with their babies attached to their bellies. During the harvesting season, at times, they ransacked the delicate vegetation and created havoc. They devoured bananas, almonds, and other things we grew for our own use.

Soon came the milkman, and then the barber

Clad in old rags, but his name was Akbar;
With rock hard soap, and a bit of water,
Demanded his wages first, shaved us later !

Adults enjoyed the shave, ear to ear,
We children harboured, a cryptic fear;
In my own mind, I dreaded him dear,
Worrying, he may just cut my ear !

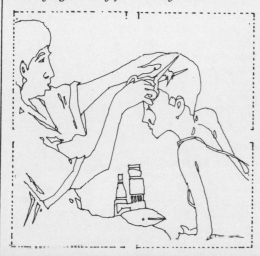

← A BARBER WITH HIS KIT paid a regular visit, door to door, typically during the morning hours. At noon, he would station himself along the roadside, ready to give a massage or a haircut to the passer-by. The aged men were his typical clientele, during these odd hours.

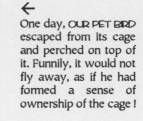

One day, OUR PET BIRD escaped from its cage and perched on top of it. Funnily, it would not fly away, as if he had formed a sense of ownership of the cage !

A certain bird, called THE GOD SPARROW, dextrous at weaving its nest with dry grass, often builds it dangling in a well, suspended from a branch of the plants growing in the crevices. It protects its family from the common predators, such as the cats and snakes. ←

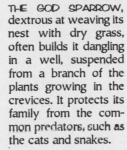

← THE VILLAGE PEOPLE gathered to sing hymns and prayers regularly. The tranquillity of the late hours helped the entire village enjoy the melody, while carrying out the activities.

→ During the festive season, children enjoyed making THE DECORATIVE MAGIC LAMPS. The colourful lamps made a glowing impression against the dark sky of the night.

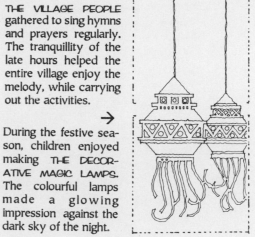

Among - the holidays, the school,

The traditions, celebrations and sights -
The holidays felt good, the school useful,
But, best was Diwali - the festival of lights.

It was a pleasure, not a burden,

Because of the closer ties;
Besides, the cows provided fresh milk,
And, the garden invited butterflies.

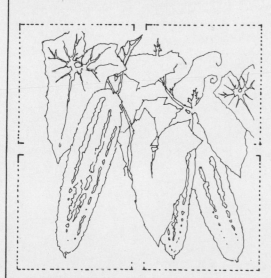

← A number of DELICIOUS CUCUMBERS grew in our garden, from September to December. Sometimes I tried to sketch them, and then, simply ate them.

THE MAJESTIC MANGO TREES provided generous shadows, which were comforting to the passers-by travelling in hot sun. ↓

During the Monsoons, the croaks of THE BULL FROGS could be heard from a distance. When approached, they remained quiet and motionless. It made it easier to sketch them. →

← Some SUNFLOWER STALKS, standing straight, showed a single sunflower each. Surprisingly, some seedlings supported several, sometimes six or seven. A sketch of a sunflower was simple because of its circular shape.

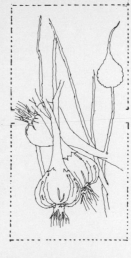

Egg plants, drumsticks, papayas and melons,

Attracted many birds, more than just once,
Blue mynahs, green parrots, black crows and ravens;
Gods probably had them not, in the garden of heavens !

THE MARKET

On every Tuesday, the local merchants from the surrounding areas brought their goods to the weekly bazaar in our village.

The market scene was a great fun for drawing amusing pictures. The whole site used to be filled with colourful merchandise and strange activities.

Women bought many bangles, of colours varied,
Besides a water pitcher, this additional load they carried,
A broken bangle to replace, the ladies always hurried,
Of all colours, green was the sign of getting married !

← THE POTS OF VARIOUS DESIGNS, displayed by the potters in the local market, was a wonderful work of talent.

← A BANGLE SELLER, with the colourful and delicate bangles in his stock, helped the buyer wear bangles on her hand. Sometimes, the seller had to squeeze her hand quite hard, in order to slide the bangles over, unbroken. The posture of the woman indicated that probably it hurt her.

← THE CHILDREN SELLING ORANGES on the roadside, when tired of waiting for a customer, often ate the fruit themselves.

Though awkward to eat, the children liked THE SUGAR CANES. Carrying them was quite cumbersome. But, it provided them ample of juice to drink.

THE FARM

My father took me to our farm quite often. Since it was not too far from our house, it was easy to go there frequently.

The tranquillity of the surrounding was broken only by the sounds of birds, animals and flowing water nearby. The farm activities presented me with several opportunities to sketch the rural life.

Early morn, prayed the Lord, then went to the farm,
Working hard, sweating in sun, caused no one any harm;
Simple food, think of Lord, before turning off the lantern,
Such was the village life, and its diurnal pattern.

THE FARMERS washed their bullocks on the river, before starting their day's work. The bullocks seemed to enjoy it, too !
↓

↑ It was interesting to draw various poses of action of THE VILLAGE WOMEN who came to the river bank to wash their clothes.

↑ At noon, while the farmers took a break for lunch, it was THE TIME TO REST FOR THEIR BULLOCKS too. A cooperative friendship was thus evident.

A SHEPHERD LOOKING AFTER HIS GOATS was often barefooted. For him it was quite natural to trod the jungle paths, so. →

THE LITTLE GIRLS helped their mothers fetch water from the wells.

THE VEGETABLE VENDORS visited the vicinity of the village, vocally vouching vigorously for their veggies.

PUTTING SHOES ON THE HOOF OF AN OX was often witnessed in the local market. First, the animal had to be fallen on the ground. Its legs had to be tied and the animal had to be held by its horns, before the shoes could be nailed to its hoofs.

A cool drink on a hot summer's day was refreshing for THE LITTLE CHILDREN who came with their parents, to the local market. Many times, they enjoyed a popsicle, called ice-fruit, prepared by mounting a lump of crushed ice on a flat bamboo stick. A coloured sweet juice sprayed over it, added to its taste.

BIG BURLEY BOYS in the bazaar, bore the bulky burlap bags of beans on their bare backs. For a bystander, the big burden on their badly bent backbones was barely believable.

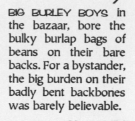

Coolie in the bazaar, was a human-jack born,
Bag of rice to him, was a bag of popcorn;
Carrying load on the back, without an ego,
Bony legs bearing it all, looked like a flamingo!

THE GOATS were excellent objects for sketching. The male goat looked very strong and dominating, but it smelled foul !

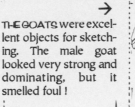

To take water out from the wells, for the irrigation purpose, an interesting technique was devised. A huge bag made of buffalo-hide was lowered into the well water. When filled, it was pulled up by THE BULLOCKS with ropes carried over pulleys.

WHILE CROSSING A STREAM, the bullocks often stopped to quench their thirst.

A STURDY CART pulled by bullocks was employed for carrying almost everything required for the agricultural purposes. When loaded full, the driver would have to sit on the yoke itself. The powerful beasts seemed to pull the load through a rugged terrain, without showing the signs of strain.

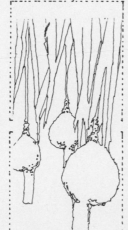

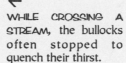

Taking water off the well, the idea wasn't revised,
With bull-power, in ancient times, the method they devised;
Immersed and pulled up, a bag of tough leather,
The land, water, animal, man, all worked together;
Gift of fresh air and warm sun, no need of a fancy coat,
The nature worked hand in hand - so the poets wrote !

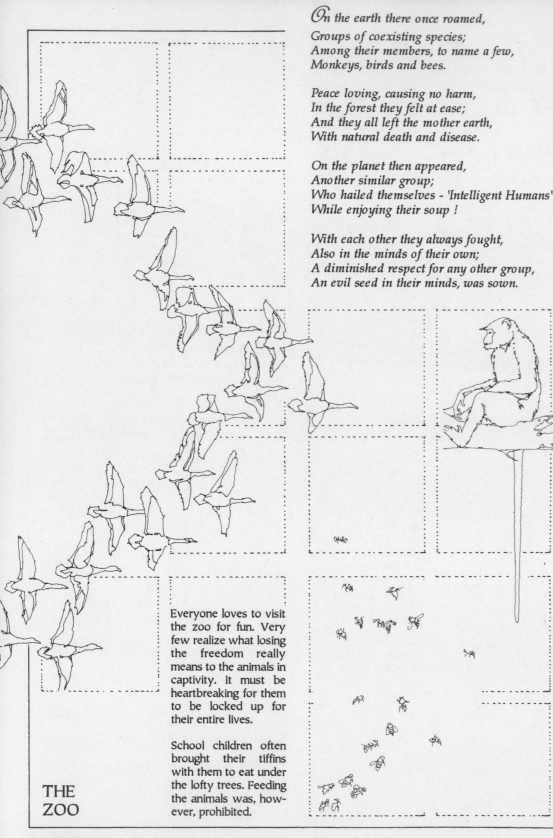

On the earth there once roamed,
Groups of coexisting species;
Among their members, to name a few,
Monkeys, birds and bees.

Peace loving, causing no harm,
In the forest they felt at ease;
And they all left the mother earth,
With natural death and disease.

On the planet then appeared,
Another similar group;
Who hailed themselves - 'Intelligent Humans'
While enjoying their soup !

With each other they always fought,
Also in the minds of their own;
A diminished respect for any other group,
An evil seed in their minds, was sown.

And then . . .

A further declaration, the humans made,
This also among themselves;
That, if any other group, did exist,
Should be treated as their slaves.

All other beings, besides their own,
Without even having a duel;
Should be assumed dangerous,
Armed, heartless and cruel !

They did not question why,
Or, how did they them so call;
In their concept of rightness, however,
They invented the name - 'Animal.'

Furthermore . . .
Meaning of this, they further defined,
As having less brain,
Less evolved, less civilized;
Without the salt or its grain !

On their minds, this they imprinted,
For themselves and their children;
He who has such opinion,
Is a member being human !

I always liked drawing a sketch of THE DEER, for the interesting dotted pattern on their coats.
↓

With this thought, did they cross,
Their so called civilized ground;
To find indeed, did exist,
A different species around !

Preconceived the 'animal' so,
With chains and ropes, them, they bound;
Pried in their affairs too,
Not the other way around !

The tricks, baits, hooks and traps,
This they called intelligence;
The demonic tendencies they disguised,
In a self-made definition of science !

Males, females of all the animals,
And their offsprings too;
The 'intelligent human' for his fun,
Rounded all of them, in the zoo !

Everyone loves to visit the zoo for fun. Very few realize what losing the freedom really means to the animals in captivity. It must be heartbreaking for them to be locked up for their entire lives.

School children often brought their tiffins with them to eat under the lofty trees. Feeding the animals was, however, prohibited.

THE ZOO

A CHEETAH had to be drawn quickly, often limiting its sketch to a mere profile. It was hardly ever steady.

→

And also . . .

Jumping across the lofty branches,
That defined the real monkeys;
In the zoo, they are kept locked,
The caretaker hiding the keys !

Again . . .

Shy birds, avoiding humans,
Crossed the limits of the skies;
In the zoo, see what the humans do,
Constantly watch them like spies !

And again . . .

Crocks and alligators, near the rivers,
Established their swamp;
In the zoo, like the abandoned boats do,
Forget they ever swam !

↑
Each pair of PIGEONS was provided its private place, called a pigeonhole. The pigeons proceeded punctually to their preassigned places, prior to a particular period. As a pastime, I practised portraying pigeons, in their peculiar poses.

Some animals, like THE GIRAFFES, displayed beautiful patterns on their bodies.
↓

Or, put it this way . . .

Snake in a straight tube, fish in a tight cube,
Exaggerated ? Yes, but isn't it suffocating ?
Locking an innocent human, behind the bars,
Why go that far ? 'know the feeling I mean !

↑
The families of THE FANCIFUL FLAMINGOS flocked freely and filled the fenced flooded fairways. The fine and flimsy feet of the flamingos felt funny from far, for, the fragile feet fulcrumed their fluffy forms full of feathers. Flamingos with their flexible necks fed on the fresh fish. Feeding the flamingos was fun, though forbidden.

A cheetah, for his speed, in the forest,
Received accolades of fame;
In the zoo, it almost looks like,
Locked in a picture frame !

Similarly . . .
The king of the beasts, in the wild,
Enjoyed the daily feast;
In the zoo, he begs humans,
"Give me the bones, at least !"

Also . . .
Magnificent elephants, having no opponents,
Roamed the forest with grace;
In the zoo, not knowing what to do,
They just scratch the ground surface !

And that is why . . .

Tell me not, that the humans thought,
Animals abjured the forest;
And settled for the zoos, in their hearts,
Having private cages and the rest !

Monkeys, birds and bees, were not born,
For their freedom to lose;
Humans will define the "animal" so,
Until they are in their shoes !

Ignoring the Gods in the heavens;
And worshipping the deity,
Destroying the nature, spreading asphalt,
Thus creating a city,
Putting an artwork in the reverse,
And then finding its beauty;
Caging the free animals, for pleasure's sake,
Isn't it truly a pity ?

CHAPTER FOUR

Scale and Proportions
... aiming for accuracy

The Deshpande Technique

After acquiring a good understanding of the concept of *basic form* of an object, the next step in the progression is to develop an understanding of the correctness of its *scale and proportions*.

For this purpose, the overall proportions in terms of the width and height of the object needs to be established. Also, the dimensions of each individual component, in relation to the overall dimensions of the object, needs to be studied carefully.

● A method of scaling an object from a distance :

A simple method to achieve the above objective was taught to us by our teacher Mr. Deshpande. With this method, a viewer can take the measurements of an object located at a distance away from him. The viewer uses his drawing pencil itself as a tool for taking and comparing the measurements. Also, for outdoor studies, which include the larger objects, such as the trees, buildings, etc., this method proves quite useful.

Exercise

Step 1

Keep an object, say a bottle, six to eight feet away from you, on a table, at your eye level.

Step 2

Hold a pencil in your right hand, if you are right-handed, so that you can slide your thumb, up or down conveniently. Make sure, your hand is fully extended straight ahead of you.

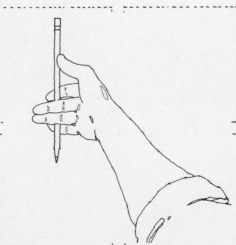

Notice that the two middle fingers support the pencil on one side, while the other two support it on the other side. This position allows the thumb to move freely up or down along the length of the pencil.

Hold the pencil vertically, straight in front of you, towards the bottle. Close one eye and position your hand so that the pencil is in the vertical centre of the bottle. Move the hand up or down, as required, to align the top of the pencil with the top of the bottle. Keep one eye closed to eliminate the double-image effect. Now you are ready to take the measurements of the bottle.

Step 3

Keeping the position of the pencil steady, slide the thumb down so that it aligns with the bottom of the cork. The length of the pencil from its top to the thumb position, representing the vertical dimension of the cork, is translated onto the pencil. The cork is the smallest individual part of the bottle, and therefore, its measurement on the pencil, may be assumed as one unit module.

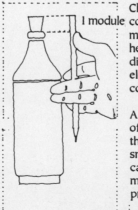

1 module

Choosing a smallest but convenient unit for measurement would help us compare the dimensions of other elements of the object correctly.

A careful observation of the bottle shows that, the cork is the smallest element that can be conveniently measured with the present technique.

Step 4

Keeping the position of the thumb steady - thereby not losing the established unit module - and moving the whole hand in downward direction, measure the length of the neck in terms of the unit just established. Say, it is three modules.

Follow the same process as above, to measure the height of the body, from the level of the neck to the bottom. Say, it is six-and-a-half modules.

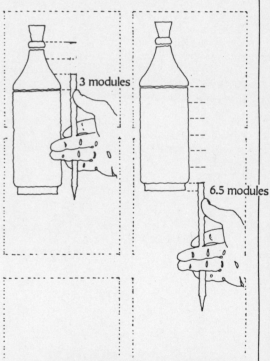

3 modules

6.5 modules

Note that, the measurement of the fractional part, in terms of the unit module, is done with judgement alone. A steady hand and a keen judgement, are essential for this purpose.

It is imperative that the position of the thumb, marking the unit length, is not changed during the entire process of taking the measurements.

Step 5

The figure shows the position of the hand holding the pencil horizontally. In this position also, the thumb can slide along the pencil, to take the required measurements.

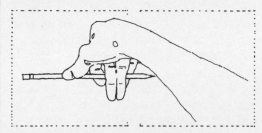

Holding the pencil horizontally, as shown, measure the width of the cork, in terms of the unit module. Say, it is one module, as shown in the figure below. Same way, measure the width of the body. Say, it is three modules, as shown.

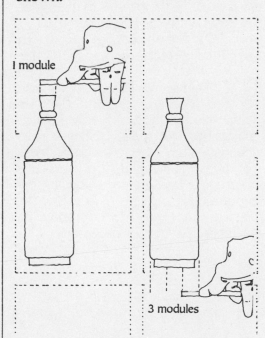

1 module

3 modules

From the above measurements, it is possible to construct a sketch of the bottle in its right proportions.

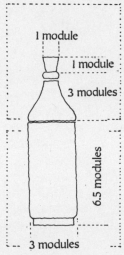

1 module

1 module

3 modules

6.5 modules

3 modules

The measurements obtained so far are summed up in the adjoining sketch.

From the comparative measurements thus obtained, the actual sketch of the bottle is drawn in the following three steps and illustrated in the corresponding three sketches below :

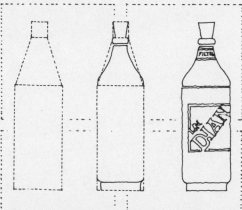

1. The basic diagram is drawn assuming the same module as established earlier.

2. The basic diagram gives a guideline, to draw the correct profile of the bottle.

3. It is now easy to add the details to the sketch. Further measurements need not be taken for this purpose.

For the purpose of convenience, hereafter, this simple technique - of scaling an object from a distance - is referred as the *Deshpande Technique*, named after Mr. H. R. Deshpande.

Once the comparative measurements are taken, it is possible to reduce or magnify the size of the sketch, simply by choosing the unit module accordingly. The technique is explained in the following section.

● Basic grid for copying a sketch to the desired size :

Superimposing a grid on the sketch helps visualize the size and the placement of each element of the sketch, instantly. Smaller the grid size, more accurate the judgement is.

Exercise

Let us assume that a figure of an Arabian ewer drawn on a sheet of paper is given to you. The exercise is to duplicate it - smaller or bigger than the original - as accurately as possible, on a separate paper.

Step 1

Draw a rectangle to enclose the given figure. All edges of the rectangle should touch the profile of the ewer. No part of the ewer should fall outside the rectangle.

Step 2

Divide the top edge of the rectangle into a convenient number of equal parts. In the sketch below, the top edge is divided into six equal modules. From these division points, draw vertical lines within the rectangle.

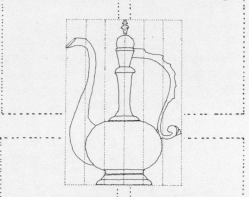

Also, divide the left vertical edge, from top to bottom, using the same module as above. It is quite likely that the remaining last division may not be a complete module. Again, from these division points, draw horizontal lines within the rectangle to form a square grid.

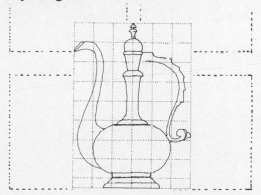

At this point, our basic grid is ready. The sketch is now divided into a number of squares of unit modules. Drawing the individual part of the object, corresponding to each module of the original sketch, is now easier, than without having the grid.

Step 3

On a separate sheet, draw two similar grids - one using a smaller and other with a bigger module. The number of squares horizontally and vertically will be same in each case, as on the original sketch.

If the last division of the grid in Step 2 was not a full unit, work out a ratio between the residual part and the unit module. Use this ratio in arriving at the lengths of the corresponding sections, in both the grids.

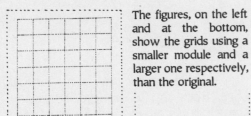

The figures, on the left and at the bottom, show the grids using a smaller module and a larger one respectively, than the original.

Step 4

Each individual square on the original drawing has a corresponding square on these two grids. Starting from top left, draw the profile of the object, as seen in each square on the original sketch, onto the corresponding module on both the grids.

Since each square contains only a small segment of the sketch, it is easy to reproduce the sketch, module by module. While reproducing each segment, from the original grid to the smaller and larger grids, a corresponding reduction or enlargement is necessary.

The profile in each module on the original sketch has a definite relationship with the four sides of the module. This relationship must be properly understood and maintained, while reproducing the segments.

At completion of all the modules, the sketch is automatically reduced on the smaller grid and enlarged on the larger grid.

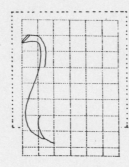

The figures, on the left and at the bottom, show the development of the profile of the ewer, in each of the corresponding grids.

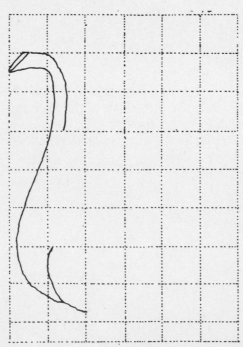

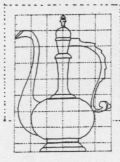

The figures, on the left and at the bottom, show the completion of the profile of the ewer, in each of the corresponding grids.

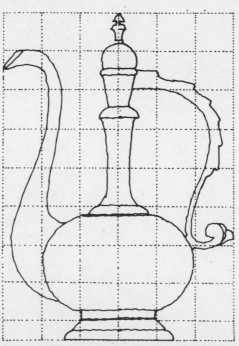

It follows that, in order to produce a sketch of the same size as the original, the size of the module used also must be same as that of the grid on the original sketch.

Practice the exercise with different sketches until you are well versed with the concept of *scale and proportions* of individual elements in relation to the overall sketch.

Often students complain that they cannot draw. What it really means is that, they have not yet developed the required sense of correct scale and proportions.

Though this exercise appears technical in a sense, it need not scare the aspirants that the artistic faculty is being reduced to a technicality. Know that, the interrelationship between various elements, in terms of their sizes and shapes, can be best understood by this method. It also acts as a facility to verify the correctness of proportions.

During my school days I used to take delight in drawing sketches with this method. Mr. Deshpande maintained that it establishes a solid foundation for learning the correctness of proportions. Sufficient practice develops a keen sense of judging the proportions correctly. Thereafter, the use of the grid, for reproducing sketches, may not be necessary.

● Completing the symmetry :

At times, there are situations that involve drawing a symmetrical object. A clear concept of *scale and proportions* is necessary to visualize the mirror image. For the purpose of practice, our teacher employed several approaches. One of his favourite methods was, to let us complete the other half of a given symmetrical design.

He purposefully chose designs consisting curved lines, to make the exercises more imaginative and challenging.

Exercise

The method of drawing a mirror image of the given design includes the following few steps.

Step 1

Study and analyze the design into its major sections.

Step 2

Select a reference point on each section, at a location furthest from the central axis. The points are located so, to get the correct idea of the extent of the bulge of each section, in the horizontal direction. The points representing the maximum bulges show the horizontal limit of each of the sections of the design.

In addition, select two more reference points on the design - one at the uppermost level of the top section and the other at the lowest level of the base section. These two points mark the limits of the design, in the vertical direction.

Using the points representing the horizontal and vertical limits, construct a rectangular frame.

Subdivide the rectangular frame, with horizontal or vertical lines, as required, to enclose each of the major components of the design.

Step 3

Duplicate the framework, including the reference points and the subdivision lines, on the other side, by measuring their distances from the central axis. These measurements could be taken simply by using the pencil itself, as a scale. The framework thus obtained sets the limits within which the mirror image fits.

Step 4

Construct the mirror image of each component, within the corresponding framework.

In our class, as we progressed, we were instructed to use fewer reference points. We were encouraged to ascertain the direction of the flow of lines, required for a mirror image, with the eye judgement alone. Consequently, I remember, over a period it became a matter of pride to draw the symmetrical objects, without using reference points.

● Directing the hand movement with mental image :

The fun of drawing, in fact, starts from the time we assimilate the concepts of basic form, and the scale and proportions.

For checking our ability in coordination of hand movement with the eye, our instructor, at the Banff School of Fine Arts, gave us the exercises to draw a sketch of an object, without looking at the sketch paper.

The aim of the exercise was to coordinate, our mental picture of the model with the corresponding required hand movement, to draw it. The teacher allowed us sufficient time. The accuracy of the sketch was not important. I found this exercise unique and very interesting.

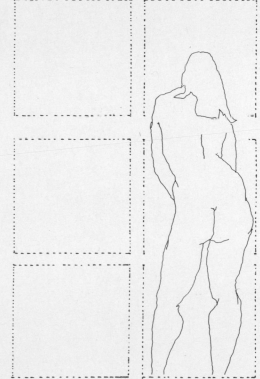

● A proper sequence
of verifying the *basic form* in terms of the *scale and proportions* :

The completion of the figure of A GIRL PLAYING MUSIC, to the extent in the Step 3 on page 8, was based on the study of the basic form. In this section, we will take the same figure to study its correctness, in the light of the *scale and proportions*.

The original figure from page 7 is reproduced below, for a quick reference.

Analyze its various components in your mind in terms of their sizes and relationship with each other.

Step 1

Establishment of the unit module :

The head of the girl is the smallest section in relation to her entire figure. Measure its height with a pencil, using the *Deshpande Technique*. Let us call this measurement as one module.

Using this as a standard module, we will compare the other measurements of the figure.

Check the width of the face. Let us say, it is also one module.

Draw a square with dotted lines, as shown in the adjoining sketch. Its width and the height should be one module each.

The entire face, with the head and the headgear, would be drawn in this square, later.

Step 2

Setting the proportions of the entire figure :

Measure the distance from the top of the headgear to the top of the pinnacle, in terms of the unit module. Let us say it is one-third module.

We must now establish the total limits of the figure, in terms of the standard module. To do this, establish the overall width, from the extreme left edge of the musical instrument to the back part of the headgear. Let us say, it is three modules.

Also, establish the overall height, from the top of the pinnacle to the bottom of the figure. Let us say, it is four-and-one-third modules, the pinnacle being one-third module.

Draw a rectangle above the headgear, one-third module high, to provide a room for the pinnacle to be drawn later. Similarly, draw the rectangular limits, as shown in the sketch, to include the entire figure. At this stage, the overall proportion of the rectangle is, three modules wide and four-and-one-third modules high.

Step 3

Scaling the musical instrument :

The position of the horizontal section, at the top of the instrument, needs to be established first.

With the standard module, check its distance from the upper rectangular limit. Let us say it is one module. Also, check its horizontal length. Let us say, it is also one module. Draw a square, one module by one module, as shown. This step establishes the critical point P, where the horizontal and the sloping part of the instrument meet each other.

The width of the remaining part of the instrument, measured from the left edge of the rectangular frame, is one module.

Now measure its vertical limits, by checking the distance from the bottom of the instrument to the bottom of the overall figure. Let us say, it is slightly more than a module, though not quite one-and-a-quarter modules.

The judgement of this fractional part, has to be done by eye alone. It is approximately one-and-one-eighth module. Draw an overall rectangle to contain the musical instrument.

Now we will determine the horizontal and vertical limits of the bell of the instrument. First measure its maximum width, from the left edge of the rectangular frame to the point at the sharpest bend. Then, establish its height, from the top of the bell to the bottom of the instrument. Also, mark the horizontal level of the point at the sharpest bend. Draw the rectangle to contain the bell, as shown.

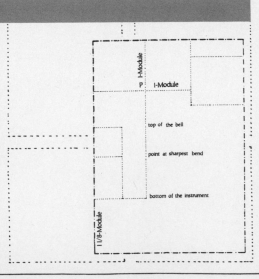

Step 4

Scaling the body section :

This step involves a careful study of the relationship of various elements of the body. It is necessary to determine the parts that fall in same horizontal level with each other, and the parts that fall in same vertical level.

Notice that the left shoulder and the top of the left hand placed on the instrument, are in the same horizontal level. This level is one-and-a-half modules, measured from the top of the overall rectangular frame. Also, establish the measurements for the bottoms of the left and the right hand.

The neck and the lowest part of the back side, as shown, are in the same vertical plane, one-third module away from the right edge of the rectangular frame. The front part of the body is one-and-a-half modules away from the right side of the rectangular frame. Draw the vertical lines indicating the above limits.

To sum up : The step involves building a rectangular frame first; and then, subdividing it into a number of sections, each representing a particular part of the object. As subdividing is based on a unit module, all parts get properly proportioned. A substantial error is thus eliminated.

Step 5

To construct the profile subsegments :

Start from the square completed in Step 1. The exercise is to construct the profiles of the head and the face, into their assigned area.

Using the *Deshpande Technique,* we find that the position of the nose of the figure is between half and one-third mod- ule long, measured along the left side of the square. Also, the front part of the head- gear is one third mod- ule long, measured horizontally along the upper side of the square.

With these compara- tive measurements, a line is drawn to indi- cate the straight line profile of the fronts of the face up to the headgear. The profiles for the head and the back part are also con- structed the same way.

In fact, during this and the subsequent steps, the profile subsegments can be built with eye judgement alone, with- out taking such com- parative measurements every time. However, the additional measure- ments do impart accu- racy to the sketch.

Step 6

Completing the figure :

Proceed to the rec- tangle at the end of Step 2, and complete the subsegments of the pinnacle on the head- gear.

Proceed to the rec- tangle at the end of Step 3, and complete the subsegments already assigned to draw the musical instrument.

Proceed to the rec- tangles at the end of Step 4, and complete the subsegments assigned for the body and the dress, as shown in the figure .

Notice that, the adjoin- ing figure on the left, with its completed subsegments, shows the following two aspects :

a.   It has been drawn to its proper basic form.

b.   Its compo- nents are verified and drawn in correct pro- portion to each other.

Attempting to draw smaller or bigger,
An object-drawing or a human figure;
An error caused, even in one part,
May make the sketch look like a modern art !

To draw an object, it must be divided,
Proportionately, further subdivided;
Its various parts neatly put together,
With correct relationship with each other.

CHAPTER FIVE

Life is short, The art long ...

Ο ΒΙΟΣ ΒΡΑΧΥΣ, Η ΔΕ ΤΕΧΝΗ ΜΑΚΡΗ
... Hippocrates
... but, patience breeds quality

At this stage, I believed that I was adequately equipped with the fundamentals necessary to sail smooth. It held good, but only in theory. If I could not draw a sketch to my satisfaction in the first few attempts, I normally gave up to start on a new subject.

I tried hard to score good results quickly, but, being unable, I became frustrated. I sensed that something was missing. It went on so, for quite a while.

Years later, I was an apprentice at Vastu-Shilpa, the office of Mr. B.V. Doshi, an architect in Ahmedabad, India. Under Mr. Doshi, I gained a good experience in drafting and architectural design.

Mr. Doshi was very amiable by nature. At the same time, when it came to hard work required for a quality product, he was quite demanding. Working around the clock was not a requirement in his office, but to meet the standards and goals he set, it was our choice to do so, in the spirit of learning. As a result of this positive attitude, we learnt that time and patience were required to attain excellence, and that the process could not be short circuited.

Precision being important for a good quality drafting, the use of delicate lines, drawn with a straightedge, was called for. I unmistakably experienced the sensitivity of pencil lines required for drafting. The softness of the pencil lead allowed variation in the characteristics of the *linework*, simply by applying different pressure. I also experienced the rigidity in the straight lines drawn with a *Rapid-o-graph*.

I was fascinated by both the media. I experienced that the straight lines, pencil or ink, had obvious limitations, when it came to drawing the sketches having curved profiles. Therefore, I decided to further explore the potential of the freehand lines, to draw sketches of all types, including the buildings.

● Mechanical Lines

A line can be drawn in more than one way. Usually it is drawn by using a mechanical means, such as a straightedge.

Any line, mechanical or hand drawn, is composed of individual sections. In the case of a mechanically drawn straight line, all sections are identically the same. Such uniform rigidity results in monotony, regardless of the line thickness.

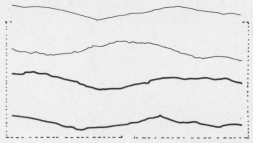

The lines, drawn with a straightedge, are used to construct the sketch of A COBWEB as shown below. The uniformity of straight lines imparts equal importance to all elements of the sketch. Thus, the major and minor elements gain equal emphasis.

● Freehand Lines

A line also can be drawn freehand. It ensures the following ingredients :

It has variations in different sections along its length. Due to this character, it appears active and full of life with suspense. Its wiggly nature indicates dancing. It reflects flexibility. It bears softness. It has breaks, knots, turns and twists. Therefore, it suggests movement and is full of magic.

The freehand lines are employed to construct the sketch of A TREE shown below. The wavy nature of the freehand lines injects flexibility, adds movement, breaks monotony, portrays softness and imparts liveliness to the sketch.

● **Drawing a freehand line :**

The character of the emerging product depends upon the speed with which the line is drawn. A constant speed should be maintained to draw lines throughout the sketch.

The adjoining illustrations show two groups of four lines each. The first group is drawn with a thin pen, while the other with a thicker pen. In each group, the first line is drawn with a very slow speed. And, the subsequent lines are drawn with a gradual increase in speed, each time. Note that, the corresponding lines do not change their character with the change in their thickness.

A sketch of A BUNCH OF GRAPES is used here for a comparative analysis of the different types of lines.

A line drawn with a very slow speed exhibits excessive shakiness and may prove disturbing to the eye.

A line drawn with a moderate speed, slightly more than the first one, possesses occasional ripples. Such line is pleasing to the eye and imparts a good quality to a sketch.

A line drawn with a slightly faster speed than the previous ones, has almost no ripple in it and bears a smoother look. It is pleasing to the eye when applied to drawing certain types of sketches only.

A line drawn with still faster speed has no ripple at all. The resulting smooth look loses the character of a freehand line. Due to the fast speed, it may terminate into an abrupt knot or a petered end and may result into sloppiness.

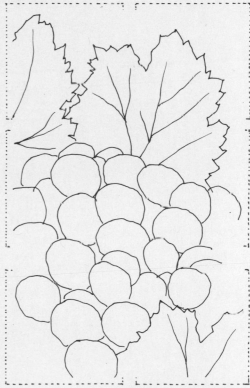

↑ Though from a distance the sketch may look same as other sketches, a close investigation reveals the weak nature of the *linework*.

The excessive ripples, as a result of the very slow speed, look amateurish and attract undue attention. It is, therefore, suggested that in this technique such should be avoided.

↑ A good quality freehand line inherits a proper balance of its straightness and the ripples. I find such *linework* most suitable for drawing sketches.

The four elements required for a good quality *linework* are :

Right pressure
Right Speed
Right terminations
Right Care

↑ The above sketch shows an absence of ripples in the lines. It is a result of the increased speed. The lines exhibit substantial smoothness.

The lines drawn faster than normal speed have a limited use. Their use in the adjoining sketch is appropriate, as they suitably portray the smoothness of the grapes.

↑ The uneven pressure and careless handling have added to the untidy character of the sketch.

The sloppy curves, unsightly endings and petering effect of the lines, are the result of an excessive speed.

The sluggishness is self evident.

● The use of broken lines

There are situations where the *linework* produced even by the finest nib is too heavy or inappropriate to express the special character of the subject matter. In such situations, the *linework*, created either with dots or small line-segments is appropriate.

In contrast with a solid line that gives a hard and committed look to the element, a broken line - dotted or segmented - imparts a less committed appearance, due to the grey-line effect.

The adjoining drawing is the on-site study of the arched passageway of THE OSIOS LUCAS MONASTERY at St. Lucas in Greece.

The side walls as well as the walls over the arches are made of a mixture of stones, bricks and brickbats of different shapes and sizes. The in fill of the clay used as mortar and the surfaces of the walls exhibit a rich texture.

If uniform lines were used for the purpose of drawing, it would not have portrayed the character of the surface texture, correctly.

←

The partial visibility of THE GROUP OF DOL-PHINS below the water surface, is aptly shown with the use of broken lines in the following sketch.

↓

● Amount of ink in the pen

If the pen runs out of ink, the *linework* becomes week and loses its uniformity. It is, therefore, recommended that the pen must be properly filled with ink at all times.

If the pen has too much ink, it may produce the lines that are too thick, and blob at times. However, this phenomenon could be turned into an advantage by an experienced hand, as can be seen in the following two sketches. A caution is necessary.

The above sketch of THE GRAPES is drawn with a *Rapid-o-graph* pen that produced an occasional blob. Much of the *linework* is uniform except that, when the pen was lifted and held for a short duration, it produced a blob.

↑
In the adjoining sketch of THE FROG, it can be seen that the blobbed *linework* has actually added an impact to the sketch.

The sketch of THE FROG is drawn with a pen that blobbed continuously. Pausing the pen at a spot produced bigger blob due to excessive flow of ink.

If the pen is overfilled by slobs,
The linework invites unexpected blobs;
Unwarranted risk such is, and hence,
Avoiding it, is a common sense.

The timing of blob is difficult to judge,
And the mistakes, thereof, are hard to fudge;
Placing them, however, with a proper feel,
The sketch assumes a unique appeal !

● A proper sequence
for developing
the segments into elements :

The Step 6 on page 20, shows the development of the *basic form* into its true *scale and proportions*, using the *Deshpande Technique*. It also explains the development of major segments into their subsegments.

After studying the *basic form* of an element within each subsegment, the detailed profile of the element can be properly drawn. Since the area of a subsegment is much smaller, than the overall size of the picture, the chances of making a substantial error are minimized. Work out the profiles of all elements to their exactness, subsegment by subsegment, carrying the sketch to its completion. The sketch will then be ready for inking.

The use of a fine tipped soft pencil - like an HB or F - to draw these profiles makes it easy to correct the errors, using a soft eraser. Keep the lines light, merely to act as a guide for the ink work to follow.

● Precaution for inking

Using a proper thickness of *Rapid-o-graph* pen, in relation to the size of the sketch, trace the elements drawn in pencil. In order to produce good quality freehand lines, establish an optimum speed required for the overall *linework*. Be careful while drawing the critical areas.

After the sketch is completely drawn with ink, use a soft eraser to rub off gently the pencil lines that may still be visible. Inkwork should be dry before erasing the pencil lines. The sketch is now ready in its final form.

Procedure for pencil-work :

Step 1

Complete the profile of the head, the hairline and the face. Be extra careful while drawing facial features. The dimensions of these features are usually very small and even a slight error, in drawing them to their correct proportions, could destroy the beauty of the sketch.

Step 2

An extra care is required to draw the lines with slopes and curves of the musical instrument The important details of the make-up of the instrument may be added to enrich the sketch.

Step 3

Draw the lines of folds in the clothing properly. Avoid the stiffness of lines while drawing these softer elements. Add a design of pattern on clothing if it helps the sketch. While drawing the hands, draw the fingers conceptually, avoiding the extraneous details.

The drawing is now ready for inking.

Procedure for inking :

Step 1

Inking should be started after the pencil work is completed.

It is a good practice to start the sketch from its top, working downwards.

Step 2

If you are a right-handed person, it helps drawing lines from left to right. It allows you to see the emerging *linework* clearly. You also may have to manipulate the speed of drawing lines to obtain the desired quality.

Step 3

Continue the process of inking with an optimum speed, avoiding the stiffness of lines. When the tracing of the whole sketch is completed, make sure that the ink is dry before erasing the pencil lines. Use a soft eraser to remove the pencil lines.

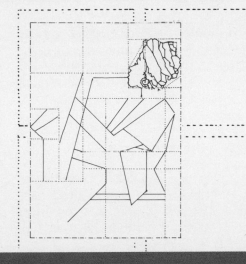

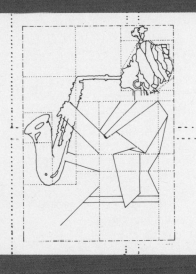

The figure at the bottom shows that :

a. It has been drawn to its proper basic form.

b. Its various components are drawn correctly, in proportion to each other.

c. All its segments are properly subdivided into subsegments.

d. The inkwork is done carefully with optimum speed.

The sketch of A GIRL PLAYING MUSIC is now ready in its final form.

A line drawn with the speed of a snail,
For an artwork, it would often fail;
Its ripples are beyond measure,
Too close together, as if under pressure;
Slow and steady wins the race,
Was not implied for this case !

Knowing the optimum speed and its variance,
Takes learning, judgement and experience;
A good freehand line one should create,
For any sketch, that is appropriate;
To practise, concentration is an ability,
For, patience breeds quality !

A line drawn faster than right speed,
Could be compared with human greed;
It may be good, but has limitation,
Overdone, may turn into poor presentation;
For any artwork, to be called - fine,
Such speed is the limit, to draw a line.

The line, if drawn still faster,
Careless and abrupt, spells disaster;
Such work portrays the rush behind,
Never use it, in the right mind;
To expect a good quality - this way -
Is like saying, Rome was built in a day !

CHAPTER SIX

Linework for drawing people
... drawing the human postures

At the Banff School of Fine Arts, Alberta, our instructor took us for outdoor studies periodically. Of the particular interest to us, was to draw people in their various poses of action.

He advised us to draw any eye-catching pose that we may encounter. For this purpose, we had to find people in their sitting or standing positions, long enough to draw a *basic form* and check its proportions quickly. In particular, places like a park, cafeteria, beach, school, etc., - were typically suitable for this purpose. The extent to

which the rough sketch could be built-up depended on how long the subject remained steady. Many times it didn't matter, as the further development and the addition of details were done later. After enough experience, we could complete the sketch with the eye judgement alone, without going through the basic steps.

In this chapter, a collection of such figures is presented for stimulating inspiration, evolving ideas and providing a handy reference.

Following the instructions of our teachers,
Out door we went, to draw earthly creatures;
Immediately though, nothing was found,
Later spotted a monkey, in the zoo around.

Among the creatures, no one surpasses,
A monkey, for its funny poses;
Looking like a man, with a tail for fun,
Monkey must be a relative of human !

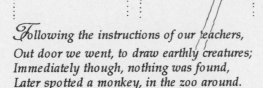

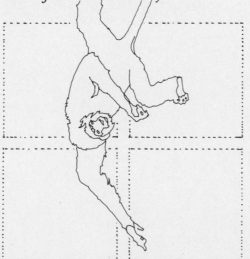

Thus . . .

The humans on the earth,
With the ever-changing poses from their birth,
Are the species, a visit worth;
To experience the outburst of mirth !

Right from the early childhood,
The imitation of monkey is pretty good;
Sometimes, looks like an aerobic art,
Humans also carry babies, near their heart.

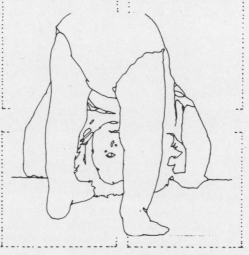

Then . . .

After a while, we went to town,
There we found, people abound;
Poses of humans, many a kind,
In a park, on a beach and school behind.

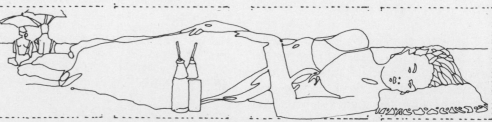

And then . . .

Males, females - younger and older,
Some carried children on the shoulder;
We saw people greeting each other,
And a baby, fondled by her mother !

And also . . .

Visited some tots with handful of Roses,
Others, in their unrecognizable poses;
Boys learning the skill, their prime duty,
On the mother's shoulder, a sleeping beauty !

Soon After ...

Under the trees were some teeny boppers,
Jumping like the grass hoppers;
For the suke of art, they quickly posed,
While others dozed, with eyes half-closed !

And yet again . . .

Nearby was a girl, wearing a headgear,
And another one, basked in an easy-chair;
Yet there were two, dancing in a pair,
And a bully with big belly, looked like a bear.

And once again . . .

Some were seen, decorating faces,
Others, tying their shoe laces;
Some kept busy, reading their essays,
And, a few simply fancied their dresses.

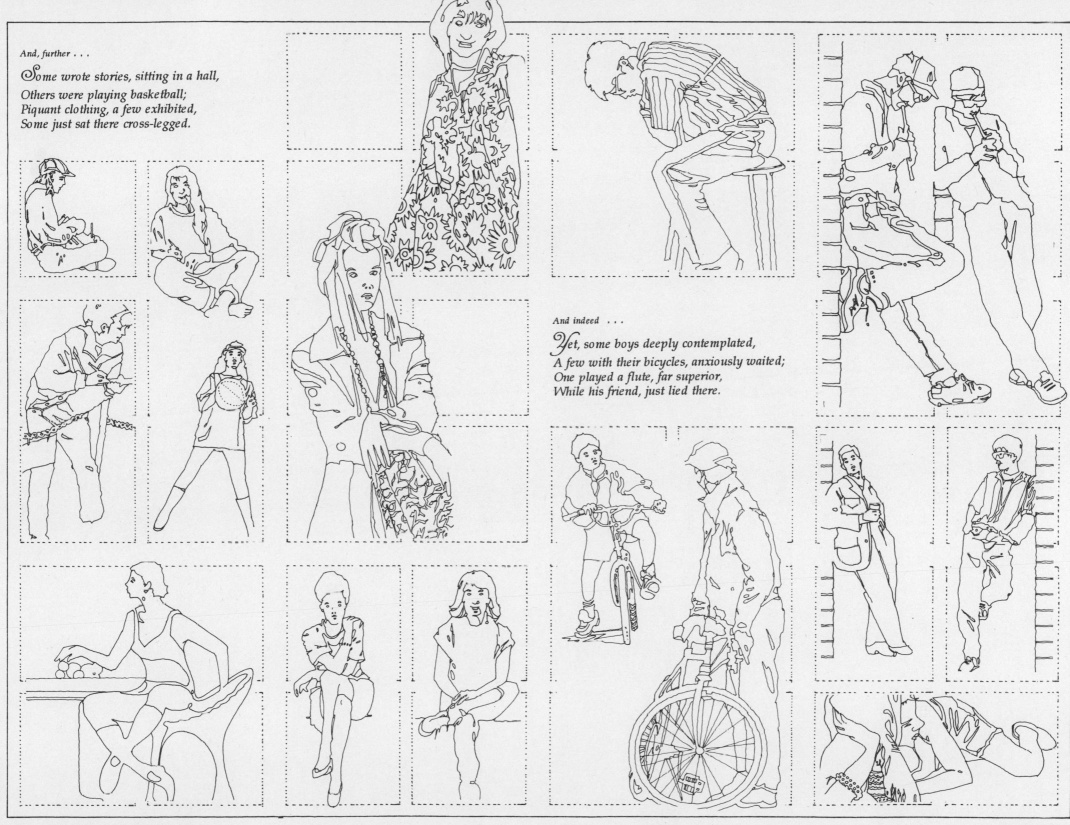

And, further . . .

*S*ome wrote stories, sitting in a hall,
Others were playing basketball;
Piquant clothing, a few exhibited,
Some just sat there cross-legged.

And indeed . . .

*Y*et, some boys deeply contemplated,
A few with their bicycles, anxiously waited;
One played a flute, far superior,
While his friend, just lied there.

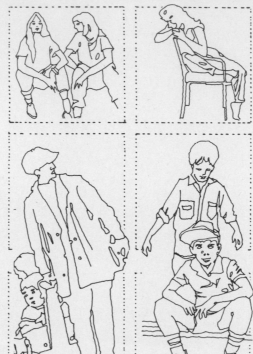

While . . .

A few looked through the camera,
Captured a picture, . . .abracadabra !
Some with friends, discussed their needs,
While others, looked after their kids.

And besides . . .

Businessmen always dressed very well,
Even in friendly meetings, they tried to sell;
When successful changed, to success debacle,
Back to hamburger, fries and dill pickle !

And lastly . . .

After drawing a number of poses,
Countless actions and body languages;
Closed my eyes, to open the inner eye,
And find my own self, where does it lie ?

I looked myself in the mirror,
Me and the image, looking at each other;
Changing poses, like a puppet show,
The real manipulator, I may never know !

CHAPTER SEVEN

Ideas and Techniques
... from A to Z

In the Seventies, I had a privilege to work with Mr. Brian Brooks, an architect in Toronto. In his association, I further learnt the proper use of *linework*, as applied to sketches.

As Brian drew an architectural sketch, I could actually sense that he had a complete image of it already worked out in his mind. And that, the lines emerging from his pen seemed to merely trace the mental picture onto the paper. The entire process seemed smooth and flawless.

I always liked to hear him comment on my sketches, architectural or otherwise. Though I felt that a sketch was complete and satisfactory, he always had a positive comment or two, to improve it. Needless to say, it helped me every time. And then I wondered, why I did not think of that aspect myself. In the process, I realised that a sketch built on a clearly expressed theme, always bares a good quality. May it be a sketch of a skyscraper or an old cottage, it is basically a work of art.

In this chapter, I have made an attempt to summarize various ideas to express a sketch. The ideas are arranged in a progressive fashion, starting with the use of a minimum lines, progressing through the use of a profuse *linework* and texture, and ending with an application of a tone.

The objective of the present approach is to make the aspirants aware of the underlying theme behind each sketch. The ideas are arranged in a logical sequence for ease of understanding. It is hoped that this approach will help them maintain an interest and help absorb the underlying principles, as each idea unfolds itself.

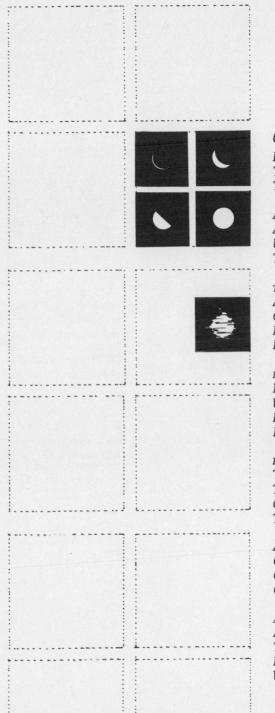

Observing the moon, in the sky clear,
I saw its profile, being part of a sphere;
The days after, was a quarter moon seen,
Then a little more, observed my eyes, keen.

A few days later, it showed its half,
Again more and more, on its behalf;
Until the full bright circle, was clearly seen,
Totally different, than what it had been !

Thereupon ...
As the day ended, by and by,
Overcome with the darkness of the sky;
Noticed I, the moon and its moods,
Its image was melted, behind the clouds.

In short ...
Nature presented the moon over fifteen days,
With its changing moods and expressive ways;
Including the sight forming a halo,
From the day 'A' through the day 'O.'

Put it this way ...
To express the moon, in a particular way,
The idea is to ascertain the day;
Once the day is fixed particularly,
The outcome is fixed, accordingly.

An example is taken of a moonlit night,
Only for a comparison, to make a point;
Concept being fixed, its expression may differ,
Call it an idea or a theme - as you prefer !

And hence ...
An idea for a sketch, once planned, similarly,
The result is obtained, accordingly;
Explained such, are the ideas ahead,
With illustrations - from A to Z.

AIMING FOR THE LEAST

Here, the theme is to draw a sketch with the least amount of *linework* and express the object in a nutshell. The essence of the subject matter is summarized by eliminating the extraneous *linework*. The good old adage - the least is the best - is the underlying idea.

● Germ of the idea

A blank canvass instigates an intense search for the eye to find something on it. Thus, attention is focused on anything that is drawn on it, even a simple dot.

In the example mentioned earlier, a single dot on the blank area attracts attention and holds it at one place. Drawing more than one dot would divide the centre of attention.

→

If the tiny dots were to represent THE STARS IN THE SKY. showing no more than just a few of them would be sufficient to convey the idea.

←

An application of the above principle is used in drawing a sketch of THE SNOW-FLIES sitting on the snow. Here the tiny bugs hold the centre of attention.

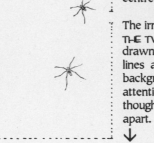

The irregular profiles of THE TWO LITTLE BIRDS. drawn with just a few lines against the large background, fix our attention on them, even though they are spaced apart.

↓

↑

Each dot in the background of THE SNOWY LANDSCAPE represents a post of the fence.

In the adjoining sketch, an intricate nature of A BRANCH OF A TREE is summed up in a few well-composed line forms.

Each line in the distant background represents a bird flying in the sky, in the adjoining sketch of THE FLYING BIRDS.

↓

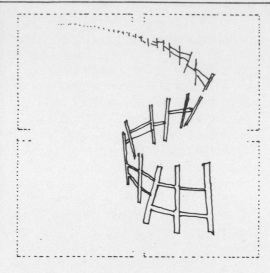

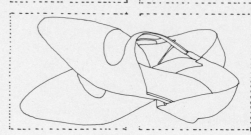

The adjoining sketches - of THE DECORATIVE GLASS BOWLS. THE FRYING PANS and A PAIR OF SANDALS - are drawn with the least number of lines.

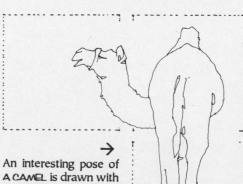

→

An interesting pose of A CAMEL is drawn with a continuous flow of lines.

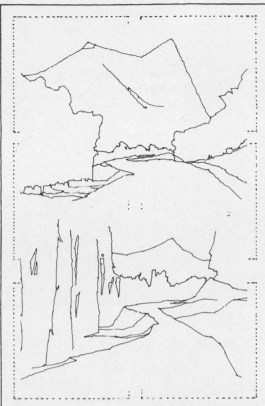

↑
Barely a few lines create an impression of A LANDSCAPE OF THE MOUNTAINSIDE, in each of the above two sketches.

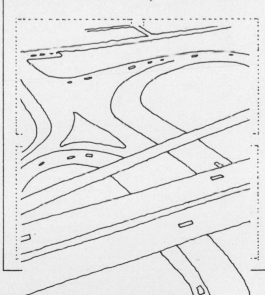

The sketch of an intricate HIGHWAY NETWORK is drawn without using too many lines. The few dots shown on the freeways are enough to suggest the movement of cars.
↓

The human figures also can be drawn with the use of a minimum number of lines. The idea is expressed in the adjoining four figures - THE TEACHER writing on a chalk board. THE LADY. THE DRUMMER, and THE BOY LOOKING BACK.

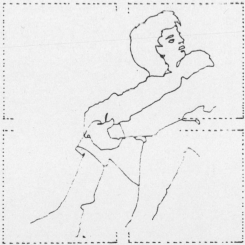

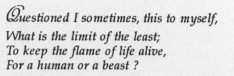

↑
An impression of the CN TOWER, Toronto, standing straight with its soaring spire, is shown simply using a minimum number of lines.

In the second sketch, shown on the right side, more *linework* is added to explain some of its salient features. The first sketch expresses its impression, while the second one elaborates it.

Questioned I sometimes, this to myself,
What is the limit of the least;
To keep the flame of life alive,
For a human or a beast ?

After years of contemplation, deep meditation,
And guided my own acumen by,
I could not avoid the basic question-
Who really am I ?

It is rightly said ...
"I have the possessions, not - I am,
I have the fame, not - I am,
I have the body, not - I am,
I am the spirit soul. Yes, I am."

The point is ...
A soul needs body, itself to express,
Likewise, a sketch needs lines, more or less;
Vulgar additions to a body are hinderance,
For a true realization of the spirit's essence.

By way of an example ...
In nature, I found, saving a soul,
When confronted with a hazard;
Was done by shedding its own tail,
By the clever lizard !

With this common sense,
It saves its essence;
Even without its tail intact,
It still remains a lizard, in fact !

Similarly,
Cutting a limb or two, does not change,
My intrinsic qualities - what I am;
So long as the heart and brain cooperate,
The soul proclaims - who I am !

Thus,
The awareness of the soul is more and more,
When the body - or sketch - is cut to its core;
No wonder, wise men say, therefore,
"The less is often more."

BALANCE BETWEEN THE LINE THICKNESSES

The choice of a particular thickness of line depends upon the size of a sketch to be drawn. Too thick or too thin lines will not produce a desired result.

Thus for any sketch, an ideal thickness of a line, i.e., the size of a pen, needs to be determined first. *A range of Rapid-o-graph pens, between the nib No. 000 and No. 1, is commonly used for most sketches.*

In certain situations, the extra thick or thin lines are deliberately introduced in order to impart a particular effect to the sketch.

● **Germ of the idea**

The elements in the following sketch of a leaf, namely - the petiole, midrib and the vein structure, are correctly portrayed by the hierarchy of thicknesses.

← In the sketch of A KAN-GAROO, a delicate appearance is rendered by using a very fine pen.

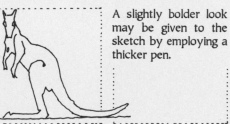

A slightly bolder look may be given to the sketch by employing a thicker pen.

At times, an emphatic sketch is obtained by using a heavy line.

Sometimes, a special effect is created by filling the sketch with a solid tone.

In the example on the right, the pattern on THE CHINESE VASE is heavily emphasised. The use of heavy lines brings out the pattern in prominence, in comparison to the rest of the vase. Thereby, it imparts a robust look to the object. The use of thicker lines, than shown, may result in a crude appearance to the vase.

In the example on the right, the pattern is drawn with thinner lines than in the previous case. A proper balance - between the thickness of the line required to draw the pattern, and the size of the object - is critical to achieve an overall pleasant look.

In the example on the right, the pattern is drawn with very thin lines. It injects softness and results in an elegant look.

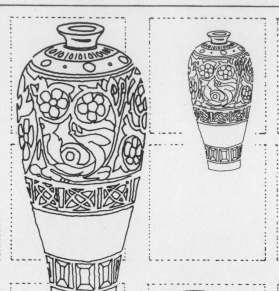

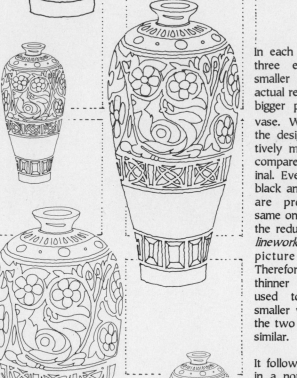

In each of the above three examples, the smaller sketch is an actual reduction of the bigger picture of the vase. When reduced, the design looks relatively more dense, as compared to the original. Even though the black and white areas are proportionately same on the large and the reduced sizes, the *linework* on the smaller picture dominates. Therefore, A relatively thinner nib must be used to draw the smaller vase, to make the two sketches look similar.

It follows that, though in a normal situation, certain thickness of a *Rapid-o-graph* nib may be the most suitable to draw a sketch, at times the use of a heavier or thinner line thickness may be required to obtain a particular effect.

The correct choice of a nib helped achieve the fineness in the adjoining sketch of THE HART HOUSE TOWER, University of Toronto. Note that, the important details of the building are shown without adding undue weight.

The sketch of A BARE TREE shows a good balance between the line thicknesses required to depict the foreground, trunks and the branching system.

On site study of the Hart House tower, University of Toronto campus.

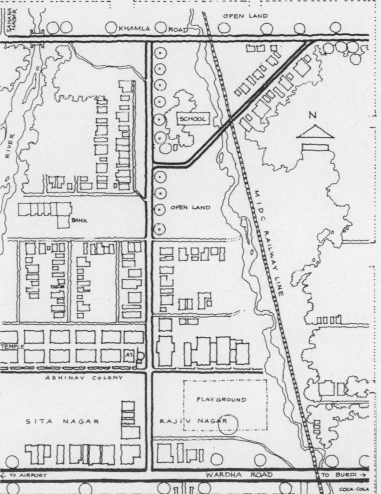

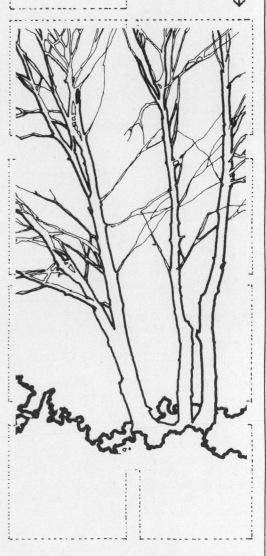

The lines of various thicknesses may be required in an artwork, such as A NEWSPAPER ADVERTISEMENT or A ROAD MAP, as shown in the adjoining sketches. The choice of the right thickness of a nib is critical in order to impart the desired weight to an individual element, in each sketch.

Related to an image of a large size,
Using thicker line is prudent and wise;
The same image, if needed small,
Comparatively speaking, that's all;
The thinner line is the need,
To draw such sketch, indeed !

CONNECTIONS AT NODES

A nodal connection - the meeting point of two or more lines - is expressed differently in different sketches. Each type of connection imparts its own characteristics to the sketch. Four such connections are shown here for a proper comparison.

Simple junctions

The junction itself is formed with lines meeting in a T-joint, as shown.

Cross connections

Here, the junction is formed by a line intersecting another, as shown.

Altering the flow of lines

The line suddenly changes the direction of its flow, giving the junction a softer quality.

Creating sections and nodes

Due to the stoppages in *linework*, the nodes are created along the path and at the junction points of the lines.

● **Simple junctions**

In a sketch where the lines meet each other in a T-joint, the connection is called a *Simple junction*. It does not create a node of special emphasis.

The adjoining sketch illustrates such line connections. It is the most commonly used technique of drawing sketches, because it imparts a finished look. ↓

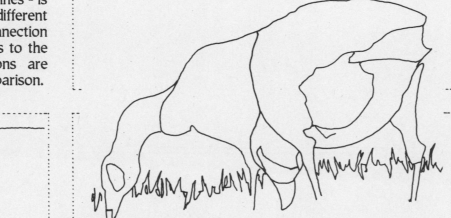

● **Cross connections**

In a sketch where a line-ending extends beyond the cross-point, the junction is called the *Cross connection*. It imparts an unfinished look to the sketch.

The adjoining sketch shows such line connections. Such crossing emphasizes the nodal connection and adds a loose appearance to the sketch. ↓

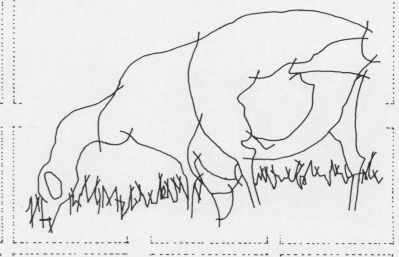

↑
● **Altering the flow of lines**

In this technique, a line suddenly changes its flow of direction at the nodal point. The visual continuity of the line is, however, maintained by commencing another line from the connection point, with a slight gap. The effect of *Altering the flow of lines* from one part to another part of the object, or, from one object to another, creates visual dynamics.

The adjoining sketch shows the use of *Altering the flow of lines*.

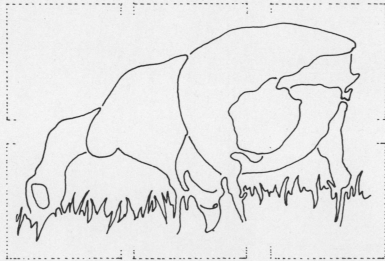

↑
● **Creating sections and nodes**

The technique involves drawing the sketch with lines composed of sections. It reveals their stoppage points and nodes.

The adjoining sketch is drawn with the technique of *Creating sections and nodes*. It reflects the sequence of drawing various parts of the sketch, and thereby adds a matured look.

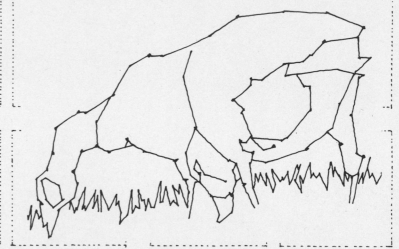

The adjoining sketches - of THE AERIAL VIEW OF THE HOUSES, and the arrangement of THE WOODEN STOOLS - show the use of *Simple junctions*.

The examples show that the connection points do not exhibit a special emphasis. The character of the nodal points itself does not add any impact to the appearance of the sketch.

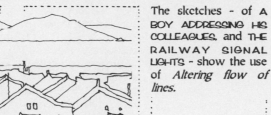

The sketches - of A BOY ADDRESSING HIS COLLEAGUES, and THE RAILWAY SIGNAL LIGHTS - show the use of *Altering flow of lines*.

The examples show that the technique helps tie the elements of the sketch together properly and thereby imparts an overall homogeneous appearance to the sketch.

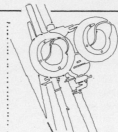
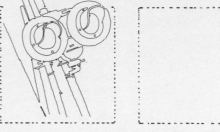

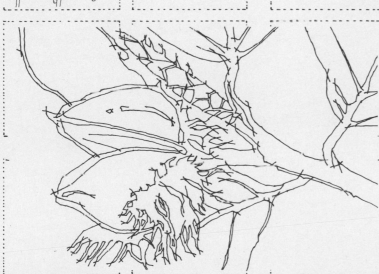

The adjoining drawings - of A YOUNG GIRL FISHING, and THE HANGING BIRD NESTS - use the technique of *Creating sections and nodes*.

From the examples it can be observed that, the form and anatomy are built with the use of sections of straight line. The sketch thus receives a mature look.

The adjoining examples - of a close up of THE BRANCH OF A TREE, and THE METAL FENCES - employ the technique of *Cross connections*.

In both examples, an unfinished look of the sketch is noticeable as a result of the open-ended lines visible throughout the sketch.

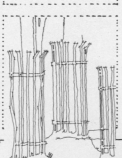

The connections of lines, create the nodes,
Of the important ones, here are a few modes;
The joints, when repeated and typified,
The sketch is thereby identified.

When a joint shows no special suggestion,
But, only a T-connection at the intersection;
The result is plain, though keeping clarity,
Like a normal man doing his daily duty.

And ...
Meeting lines, at times, forming a cross,
Sometimes suggest a gain, sometimes a loss;
Open-ended lines have their own claim,
If a casual look for the sketch, is the final aim.

And also ...
The technique of Altering the flow of lines,
Is like the joints of the railway lines;
A sudden change of direction, warning free,
Softens the sketch to a large degree.

And again ...
Drawing the object in line-sections,
Studying its form, anatomy and composition;
Also, when nodes are expressively shown,
Attains the sketch, a quality of its own !

DEPICTING WITH DOUBLE LINES

A slight exaggeration of the thickness of an element is sometimes presented with a double line, to add a healthy appearance to the sketch.

● Germ of the idea

A proper choice of space between the double line is required to convey the necessary strength of the element.

The sketch shows A REAR SECTION OF A PARKED BICYCLE. In this sketch, the spokes of a bicycle wheel are drawn with a single-line thickness. Though the thickness of these fine lines is shown proportionately correct, it does not convey the strength required to support the wheel. The spokes therefore look weak.

↓

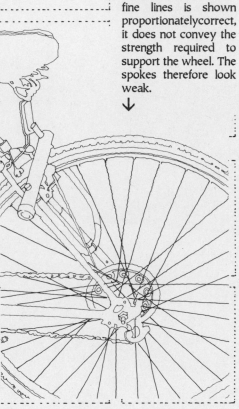

The second sketch shows the use of double lines to draw the same elements. By showing the spokes with double lines, their thickness is slightly exaggerated. However, the added thickness gives a good dimension to the spokes that results in a proper visual balance to the wheel. The use of double lines is appropriate here.

↓

The third sketch is also drawn with double lines maintaining the same spacing but using a thicker nib, than used for the previous sketch. The further addition of thickness to the spokes takes away the fineness of the spokes. Consequently, the extra thickness makes the spokes look too sturdy for a bicycle wheel.

↓

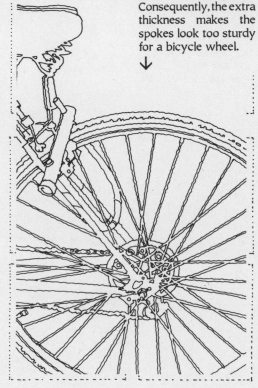

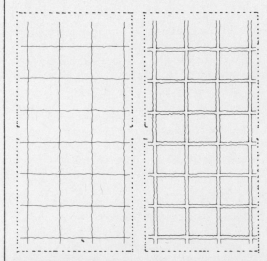

→

A DECORATIVE MOTIF from Egypt, is portrayed with the use of a number of double lines with an appropriate space between them.

Note that the strength of the sketch would not be the same, if a single line approach was used, instead.

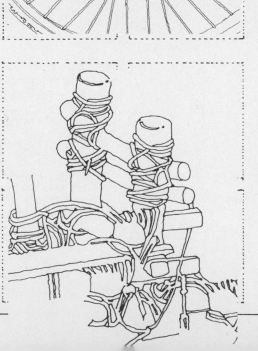

←

The sketch of THE ROPE, shown with double lines, carries the idea of the strength required to tie the posts firmly. The same construction shown with single lines would not convey the idea properly.

→

Though made of thin wires, the character of AN UMBRELLA CADDY is correctly depicted by exaggerating the thickness of wires.

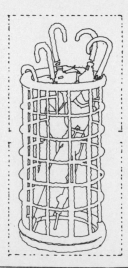

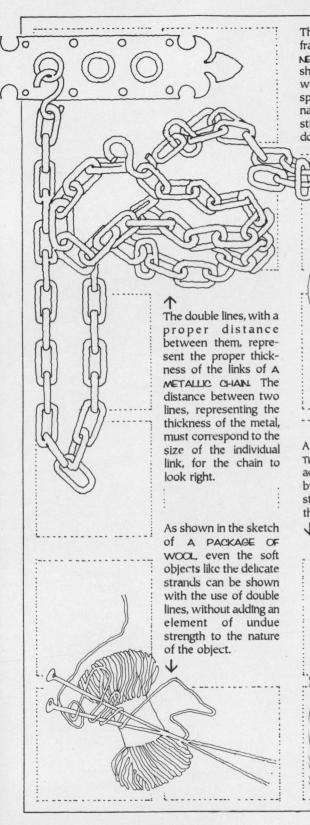

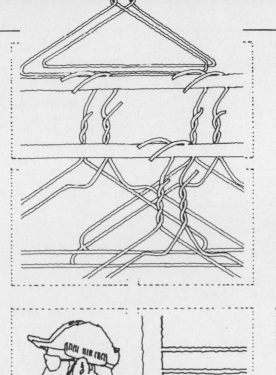

The sketch of the framework of THE CHINESE LIGHT SHADES shows the ribs drawn with double lines. In spite of the fragile nature of the bamboo sticks, the use of double lines to exaggerate slightly their thickness, helps the sketch look healthy. →

The use of double lines allows a proper representation of THE COMMON COAT HANGERS.

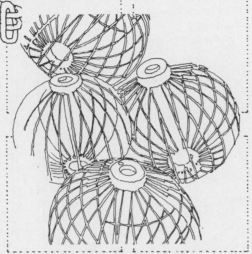

↑ The double lines, with a proper distance between them, represent the proper thickness of the links of A METALLIC CHAIN. The distance between two lines, representing the thickness of the metal, must correspond to the size of the individual link, for the chain to look right.

A uniform thickness for THE METAL WIRE is achieved in the sketch by maintaining a constant distance between the double lines. ↓

As shown in the sketch of A PACKAGE OF WOOL, even the soft objects like the delicate strands can be shown with the use of double lines, without adding an element of undue strength to the nature of the object. ↓

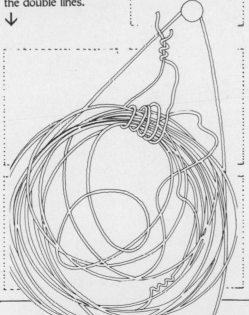

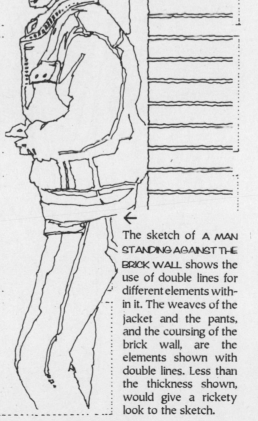

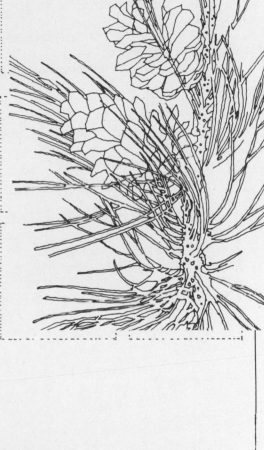

The sketch of A MAN STANDING AGAINST THE BRICK WALL shows the use of double lines for different elements within it. The weaves of the jacket and the pants, and the coursing of the brick wall, are the elements shown with double lines. Less than the thickness shown, would give a rickety look to the sketch.

Unless the object is extremely fine,
Like a hair of a swine, or a spider's line;
Using two lines - with a space - in between,
Is appropriate, in the cases nine out of nine !

Therefore ...
When the thickness of an object isn't very fine,
Like the twig of a vine, or a needle of pine;
May it be straight, curved or combine,
Consider drawing it with a double-line.

EMPHASIZING WITH HEAVY LINES

Lines of more than one thickness are sometimes employed to create a contrast or to emphasize a particular element, within the sketch.

However, if the lines are too thick, or if the proper balance of lines is not achieved, the eye gets caught up by the thickness of the heavy *linework* itself, more than the clear perception of the overall image. The weight of *linework* should not overpower the clear identification of the sketch.

● **Germ of the idea**

A combination of thin and thick lines, generates a play of contrast between the line thicknesses. The glitter in the sketch is created as a result of the placement of lines of different thicknesses side by side. The eye finds it amusing to relate the lines of different thicknesses when juxtaposed.

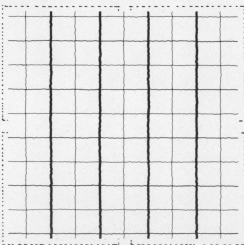

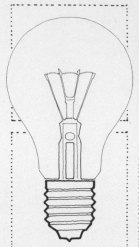

← The thin line outlining the profile of THE ELECTRIC BULB aptly reflects the transparent and delicate qualities of glass, whereas the thick line employed to draw the metal base correctly depicts its comparatively harder surface.

In the sketch of AN OLD MANSION, the tree in the foreground is brought out by drawing it with heavy lines. The house in the background, drawn with thinner lines, creates an interesting contrast with the tree. The tree looks closer to the observer while the house appears further away. ↓

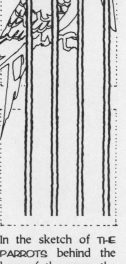

In the sketch of THE PARROTS behind the bars of the cage, the contrast between the two line thicknesses creates an illusion of distance between the cage and the birds behind.

A heavy line is used for drawing only the profile of THE BOYS PLAYING BASEBALL. The rest of the *linework* is kept within the boundary of the profile. It contributes to the contained appearance of the sketch.

In the sketch of THE HANDBAGS, the heavy line ties the elements together in a tight format. They also help emphasize the residual areas.

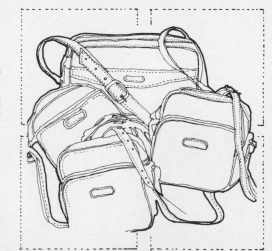

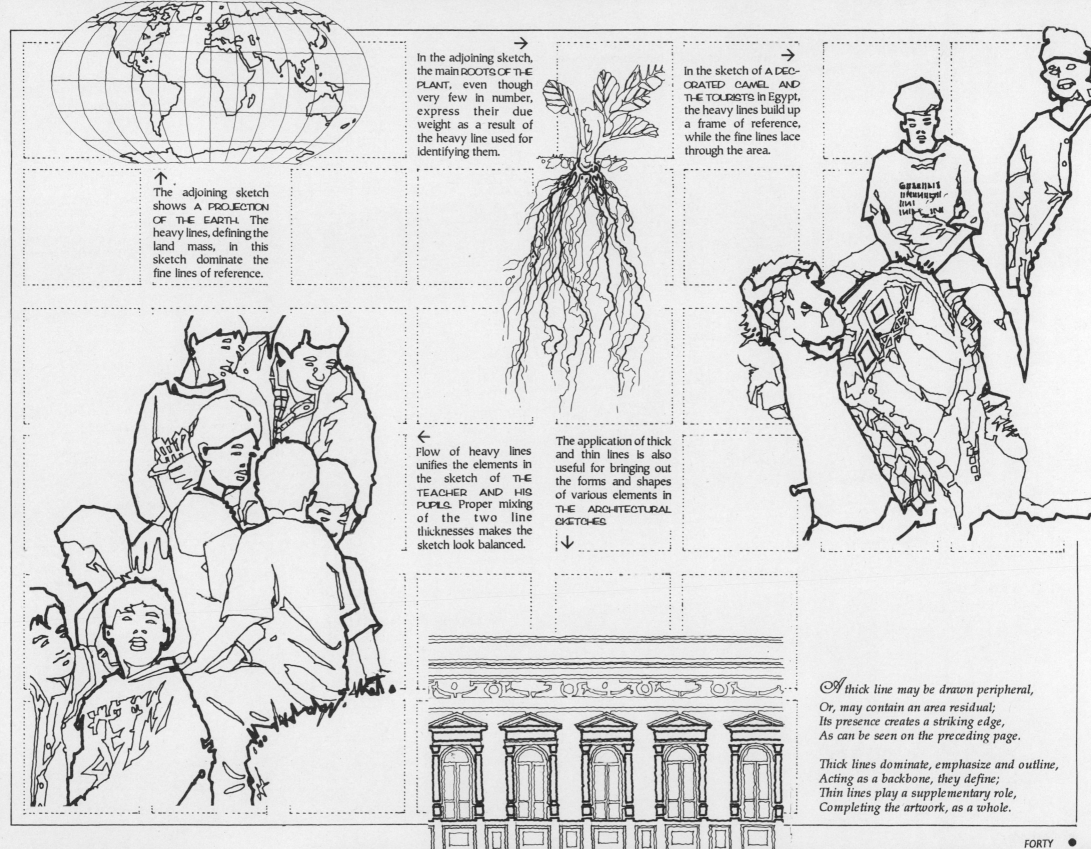

↑ The adjoining sketch shows A PROJECTION OF THE EARTH. The heavy lines, defining the land mass, in this sketch dominate the fine lines of reference.

→ In the adjoining sketch, the main ROOTS OF THE PLANT, even though very few in number, express their due weight as a result of the heavy line used for identifying them.

→ In the sketch of A DECORATED CAMEL AND THE TOURISTS in Egypt, the heavy lines build up a frame of reference, while the fine lines lace through the area.

← Flow of heavy lines unifies the elements in the sketch of THE TEACHER AND HIS PUPILS. Proper mixing of the two line thicknesses makes the sketch look balanced.

The application of thick and thin lines is also useful for bringing out the forms and shapes of various elements in THE ARCHITECTURAL SKETCHES ↓

A thick line may be drawn peripheral,
Or, may contain an area residual;
Its presence creates a striking edge,
As can be seen on the preceding page.

Thick lines dominate, emphasize and outline,
Acting as a backbone, they define;
Thin lines play a supplementary role,
Completing the artwork, as a whole.

FLOW OF HEAVY LINES

The technique of altering the flow of a heavy line within the sketch, can be effectively employed to create a special effect.

● **Germ of the idea**

The sudden change in the flow of direction of a heavy line triggers dynamism. At the same time, it ties the elements of the sketch together. The technique adds zest to the sketch.

In the adjoining sketch of THE GROUP OF TREES, the random flow of the heavy lines guides the eye to travel from place to place.

The path of heavy lines along the branching system of the tree is so designed that it weaves itself well throughout the sketch.

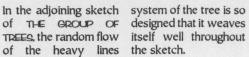

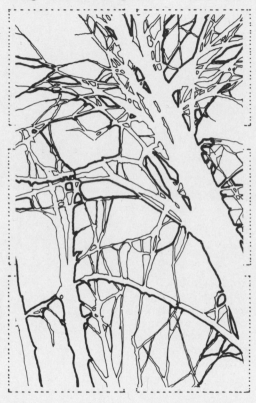

→

The heavy lines are at times chosen to highlight only some parts of the sketch. The profiles of the face and the body are highlighted at places, in the sketch of THE TWO BOYS.

←

In the adjoining sketch of THE COMMON UTENSILS, the use of altering flow of heavy lines to draw the profiles, adds a strength to the sketch. It helps break the monotony typical of the rigid profiles of the geometric shapes.

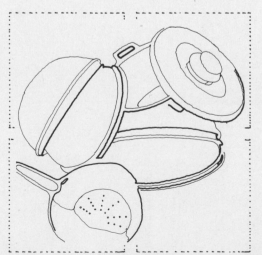

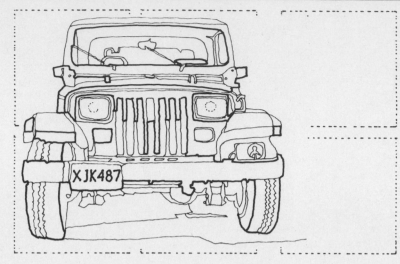

←

A meandering heavy line can be employed to lead the eye from one part of the sketch to the other, in order to add an interest. In the sketch of THE AUTOMOBILE, the heavy line flowing through the profiles of the tires, the bumper, the grill, the hood and the top, adds weight to these elements and a glitter to the overall appearance of the sketch.

The shift of a heavy line from one part to the other within the sketch is utilized to create an abstract profile, in the sketch of THE BUNCH OF ROSES. The contrast created by the heavy line, against the delicate details, helps highlight the delicacy of the elements in turn.

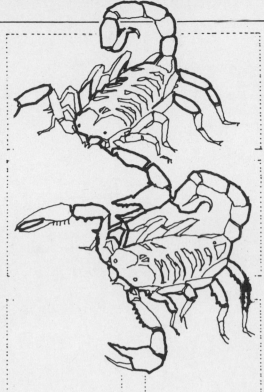

The application of the serpentine heavy line, flowing from one sketch to another, is illustrated in the adjoining example of TWO SCORPIONS. It helps the group of two individual objects tie together visually.

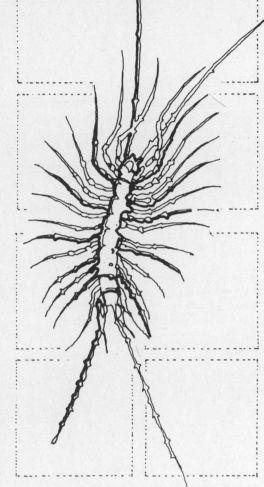

The sketch of A CENTIPEDE shows how an irregular flow of heavy lines can help add strength to the sketch, and still maintain its clarity.

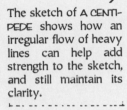

The above sketch of TWO ZEBRAS is drawn with the lines of one thickness.

Alternatively, on the left, the same sketch is drawn again with a combination of thick and thin lines to reinforce some of its elements. The confusion of the thick and thin lines, create an interesting puzzle for the eye to search for the profiles of the animals and their patterns.

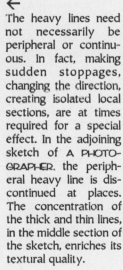
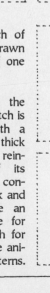

The heavy lines need not necessarily be peripheral or continuous. In fact, making sudden stoppages, changing the direction, creating isolated local sections, are at times required for a special effect. In the adjoining sketch of A PHOTOGRAPHER, the peripheral heavy line is discontinued at places. The concentration of the thick and thin lines, in the middle section of the sketch, enriches its textural quality.

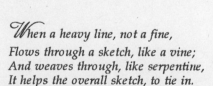

When a heavy line, not a fine,
Flows through a sketch, like a vine;
And weaves through, like serpentine,
It helps the overall sketch, to tie in.

When two thicknesses combine,
That of a thick and a thin line;
Heavy line, drawn with an irregular flow,
Imparts the sketch, a definite glow.

GUARDING THE SPEED FOR QUALITY

A uniform speed should be maintained while drawing the sketch. A proper coordination, of the correct speed and a concentration on the emerging product, results into a good quality artwork.

A delicate handling of the fine pen is evident in the slowly drawn sketch of A DRY TREE.

↓

The use of a fine pen to draw THE CUTLERY makes this tiny example a work of good quality.

↓

→

To maintain the uniformity of appearance, the sketch of the loons on THE CANADIAN DOLLAR COINS is drawn slowly with patience.

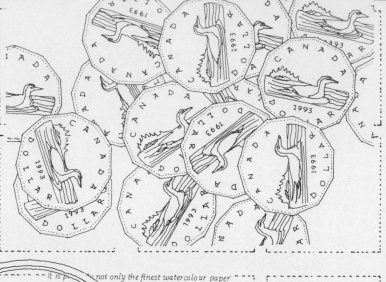

It is probably not only the finest watercolour paper you have ever used, but also the most versatile, meeting the most exacting demands of whatever technique you choose.

It is cylinder mould made, which gives stability and resistance to cockling, and a pleasing aesthetic appearance imparted from special woolen felts.

THE NATIONAL BALLET CANADA

ARTISTIC LICENCE
The Royal Watercolour Society's seal of approval

The Royal Watercolour Society's support for this traditional medium has brought it international acclaim and has led to the finest contemporary watercolour exhibitions.

Its membership has included many distinguished names, such as Peter de Wint, John Singer Sargent and Samuel Palmer.

←

In the adjoining example, three different nib sizes are used to draw the sketch of AN ADVERTISEMENT. Notice the quality of lettering achieved by drawing them slowly and carefully.

←

Drawing the sketch slowly, contemplating on each element, helps elaborate the details properly. In the adjoining example of A BOY READING A BOOK, the details of the pattern on his shirt, the texture of the grass, and the design of the fence - are drawn carefully to reflect on the quality of the sketch.

←

A slightly faster speed than normal produced the smoothness required to portray the vein structure of a RADISH PLANT.

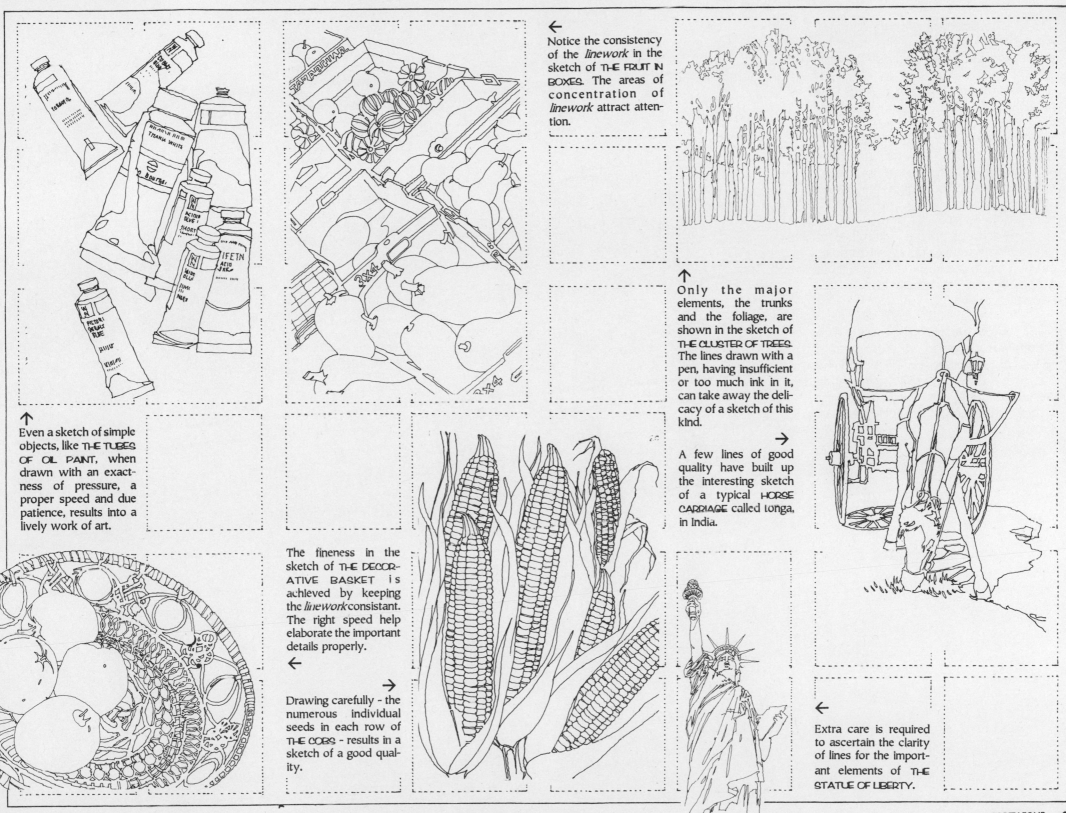

← Notice the consistency of the *linework* in the sketch of THE FRUIT IN BOXES. The areas of concentration of *linework* attract attention.

↑ Only the major elements, the trunks and the foliage, are shown in the sketch of THE CLUSTER OF TREES. The lines drawn with a pen, having insufficient or too much ink in it, can take away the delicacy of a sketch of this kind.

→ A few lines of good quality have built up the interesting sketch of a typical HORSE CARRIAGE called tonga, in India.

↑ Even a sketch of simple objects, like THE TUBES OF OIL PAINT, when drawn with an exactness of pressure, a proper speed and due patience, results into a lively work of art.

The fineness in the sketch of THE DECORATIVE BASKET is achieved by keeping the *linework* consistant. The right speed help elaborate the important details properly. ←

→ Drawing carefully - the numerous individual seeds in each row of THE COBS - results in a sketch of a good quality.

← Extra care is required to ascertain the clarity of lines for the important elements of THE STATUE OF LIBERTY.

The sketches of more complex nature are illustrated on this page, for a careful investigation of their *linework*.

In order to give a correct idea of the quality of the original *linework*, the four largest sketches - THE THORNY BUSH, THE TWO TREES, THE ENTRANCE OF A HISTORIC BUILDING and THE DRAGONFLIES - are presented here in the size in which they were originally drawn.

Each of these sketches is reduced to a smaller size also, to point out that the reduction in size results in crispness and, at times, in a better appearance.

Each of the large sketches shown here, is drawn with an optimum speed, as explained on page 22. The lines were drawn simply by touching the nib to the paper, but not pressing it, in an effort to get a good quality of *linework*.

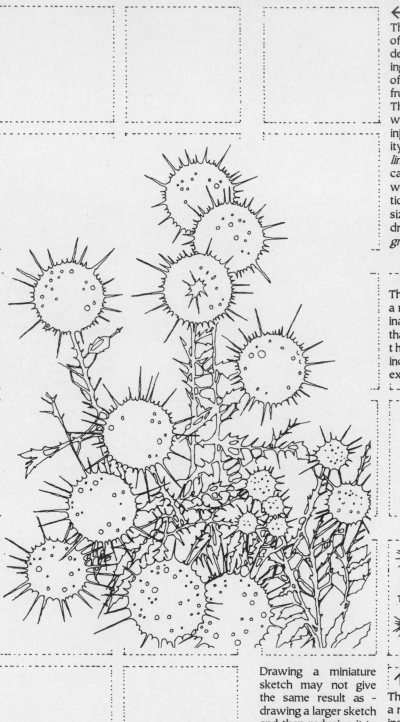

← The prickly character of THE THORNY BUSH is depicted by accentuating the pointed profiles of its needles on the fruit as well as leaves. The sketch was drawn with slow speed to inject the desired quality to its elements. The *linework* is exactly as it came out of the pen, without any magnification or reduction in its size. The sketch was drawn with a *Rapid-o-graph* nib No. 00.

→ The adjoining sketch is a reduction of the original, to 75%. Observe that, the sharpness of the sketch has increased, to some extent.

The adjoining sketch is a reduction of the original, to 50%. Notice that, the sharpness of the sketch has further increased.
↓

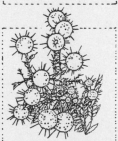

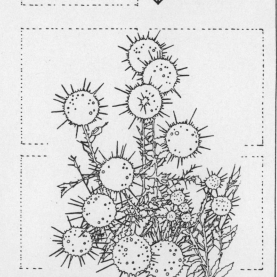

Drawing a miniature sketch may not give the same result as - drawing a larger sketch and then reducing it to the miniature size. Control over hand is difficult while drawing the tiny sketches.

↑ The adjoining sketch is a reduction of the original, to 25%. Again notice that, the sketch has further improved in its sharpness and also changed its density.

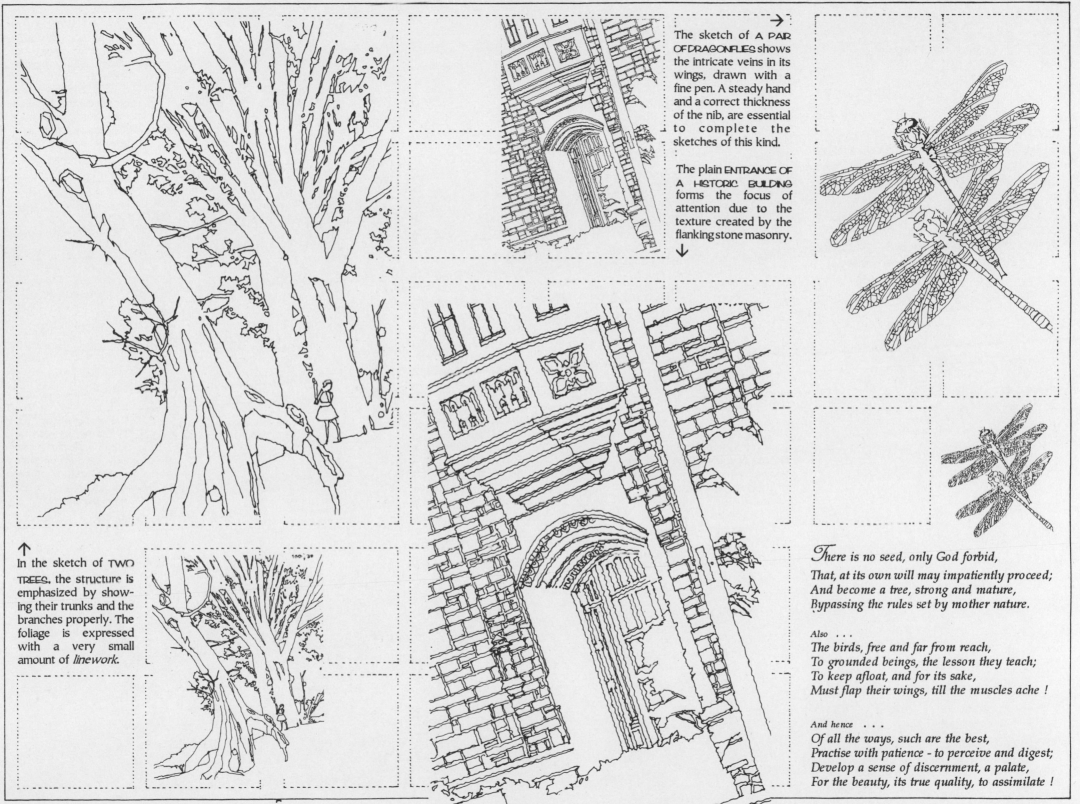

The sketch of A PAIR OF DRAGONFLIES shows the intricate veins in its wings, drawn with a fine pen. A steady hand and a correct thickness of the nib, are essential to complete the sketches of this kind.

The plain ENTRANCE OF A HISTORIC BUILDING forms the focus of attention due to the texture created by the flanking stone masonry.

In the sketch of TWO TREES, the structure is emphasized by showing their trunks and the branches properly. The foliage is expressed with a very small amount of *linework*.

There is no seed, only God forbid,
That, at its own will may impatiently proceed;
And become a tree, strong and mature,
Bypassing the rules set by mother nature.

Also . . .
The birds, free and far from reach,
To grounded beings, the lesson they teach;
To keep afloat, and for its sake,
Must flap their wings, till the muscles ache !

And hence . . .
Of all the ways, such are the best,
Practise with patience - to perceive and digest;
Develop a sense of discernment, a palate,
For the beauty, its true quality, to assimilate !

HAVING THE RIGHT AMOUNT OF LINEWORK

The amount of *linework* used depends upon the nature of the object to be sketched.

If the object is soft or plain, it should be drawn with fewer lines. If roughness is the character, a generous use of *linework* may be necessary.

The delicate appearance and the rounded shape of THE LIGHT BULBS, are expressed with a few curved lines. In a plain sketch, like this one, addition of extra lines may take away the simplicity of the *basic form* of the object.
↓

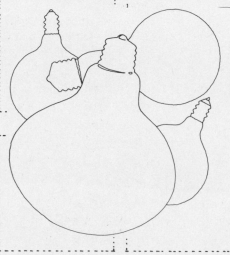

Only the important features of THE WOMAN SITTING IN A CHAIR, are shown by keeping control over the amount of *linework*.
↓

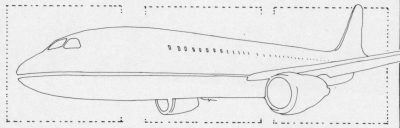

A streamlined profile of AN AIRLINER with its major components, is expressed with optimum *linework*, deleting the superfluous details. In spite of omitting the intricate details, the sketch does not appear incomplete.

A moderate amount of *linework* is required to draw THE FLOWERS. The leaves, however, need a little more of it.
↓

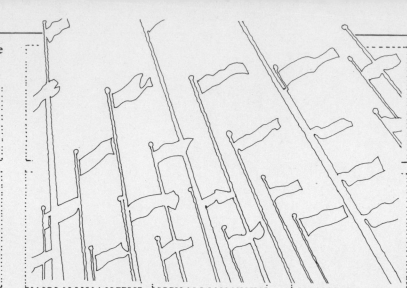

← THE ARRAY OF FLAGS with their poles is shown with a minimal *linework*. Any additional *linework* may not necessarily improve the sketch but may take away its delicate quality.

The profile of the face of THE LITTLE GIRL is drawn with just a few lines. However, the coarse texture of her hair warrants much more *linework*.
↓

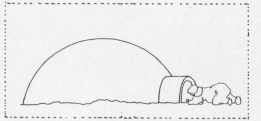

↑ Only a couple of lines are enough to draw a quick sketch of AN IGLOO.

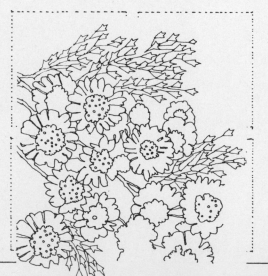

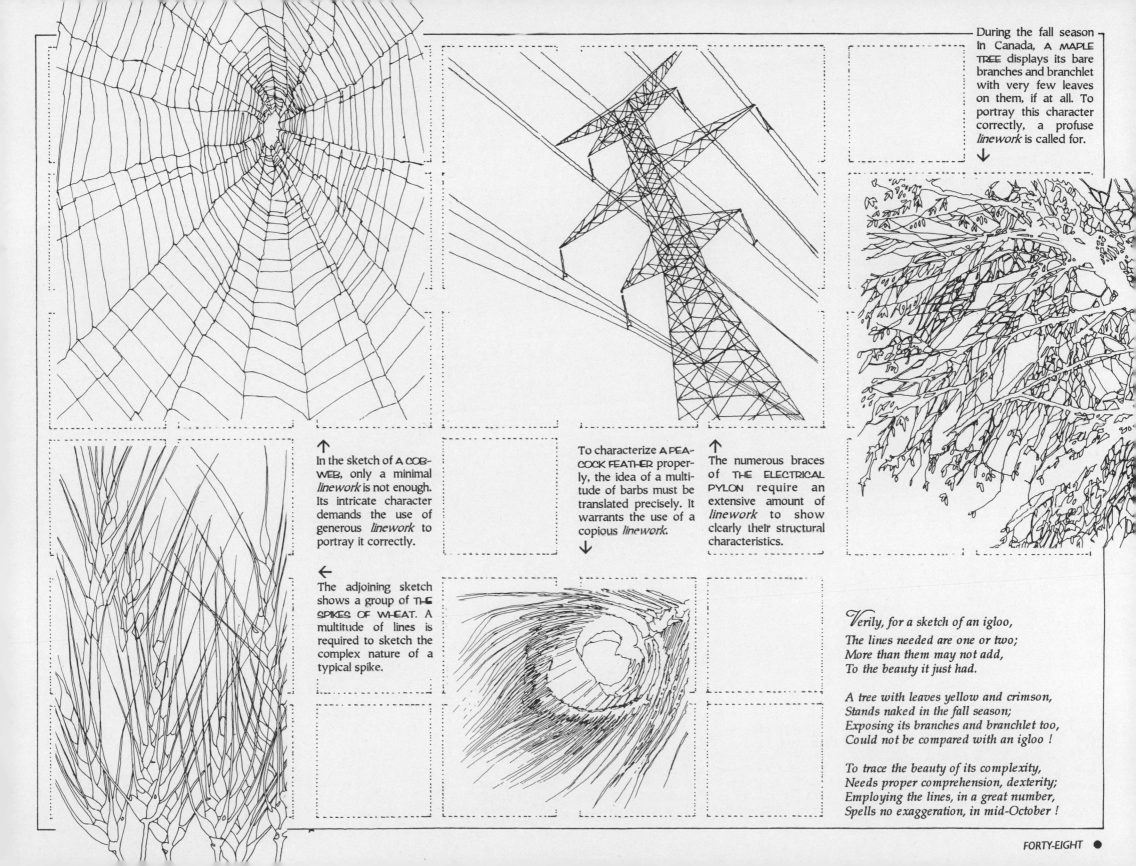

During the fall season in Canada, A MAPLE TREE displays its bare branches and branchlet with very few leaves on them, if at all. To portray this character correctly, a profuse *linework* is called for.
↓

↑ In the sketch of A COB-WEB, only a minimal *linework* is not enough. Its intricate character demands the use of generous *linework* to portray it correctly.

To characterize A PEA-COCK FEATHER proper-ly, the idea of a multi-tude of barbs must be translated precisely. It warrants the use of a copious *linework*.
↓

↑ The numerous braces of THE ELECTRICAL PYLON require an extensive amount of *linework* to show clearly their structural characteristics.

← The adjoining sketch shows a group of THE SPIKES OF WHEAT. A multitude of lines is required to sketch the complex nature of a typical spike.

Verily, for a sketch of an igloo,
The lines needed are one or two;
More than them may not add,
To the beauty it just had.

A tree with leaves yellow and crimson,
Stands naked in the fall season;
Exposing its branches and branchlet too,
Could not be compared with an igloo !

To trace the beauty of its complexity,
Needs proper comprehension, dexterity;
Employing the lines, in a great number,
Spells no exaggeration, in mid-October !

IMPORTANCE OF TEXTURE

The amount of texture in a sketch depends upon the surface characteristics of the object to be drawn.

If the softness is the aim, the object should be drawn with very little texture, if at all. The amount of *linework* builds up the textural quality in a sketch.

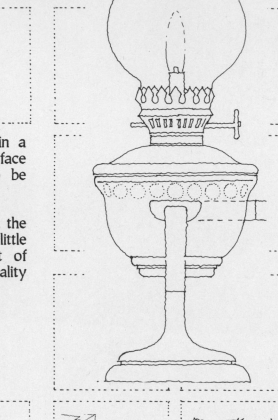

← A KEROSENE LAMP has a plain but elegant curved profile both for its body and the glass. However, the burner, in which the glass rests, has an interesting ornamental design. Thus, only the part with the concentration of *linework*, indicating the design, suggests the idea of texture.

→ In the adjoining sketch of THE GIRL DRINKING COLA, the pattern on her clothing gives an opportunity to add texture to the sketch.

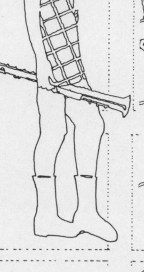

↑ Texture of THE HORSE'S MANE is the strong element in the above sketch. The abundance of texture obtained by the concentration of *linework* is limited to one area only.

The construction of THE BASKETS is shown only in some areas of the sketch. In other parts, only a few lines are enough to suggest the idea of the weave throughout. ↓

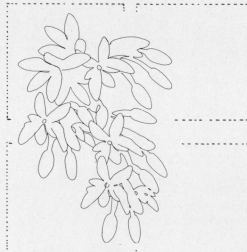

↑ The absence of texture is evident in the adjoining example of A BUNCH OF JASMINE FLOWERS. Softness of the flowers is aptly expressed by merely drawing their profile, without any texture.

↑ In the adjoining sketch of TWO GOATS, an interest is created in sporadic areas due to the texture borne by the beards and the horns of the animals.

↑ The sketch of THE BARBED WIRES shows the uniformity of texture. However, the spots of texture created by the barbs add an interest to the sketch.

→ The area of texture, expressing THE NEST BETWEEN TWO BIRDS, ties the sketch together. Since the birds have very little texture on them, the nest becomes the focus of attention.

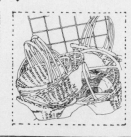

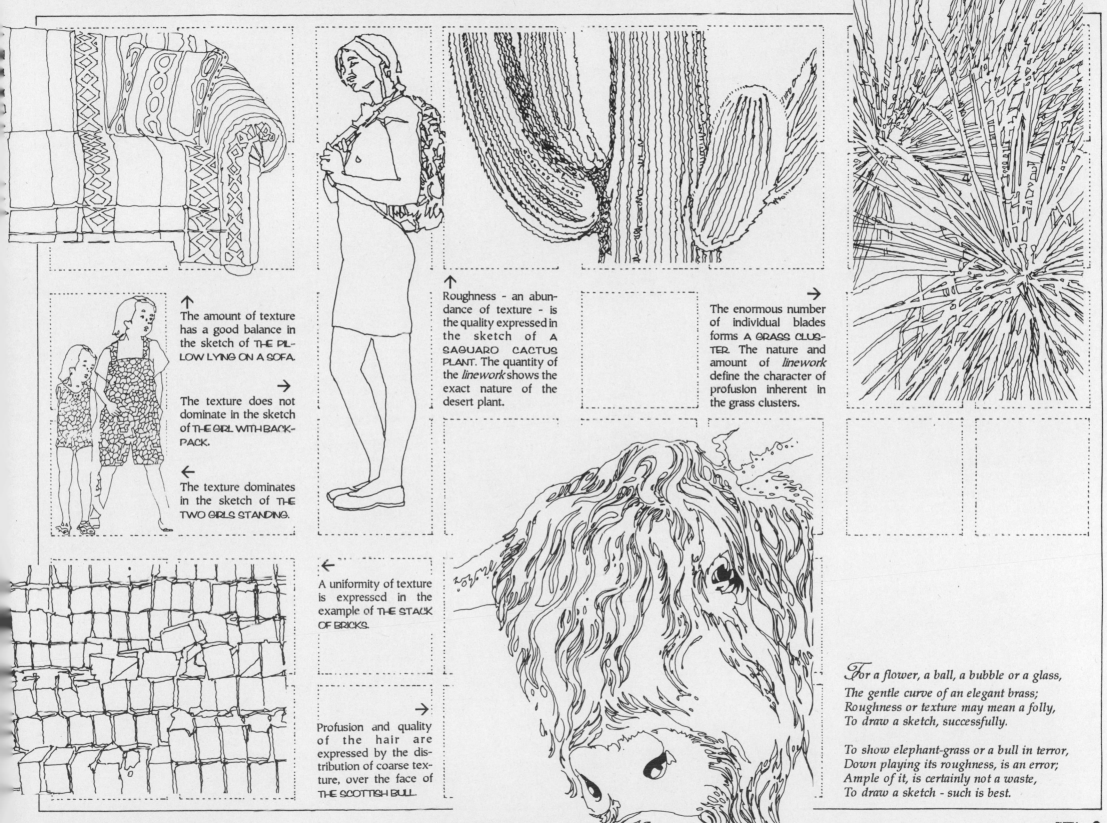

The amount of texture has a good balance in the sketch of THE PILLOW LYING ON A SOFA.

→

The texture does not dominate in the sketch of THE GIRL WITH BACK-PACK.

←

The texture dominates in the sketch of THE TWO GIRLS STANDING.

↑

Roughness - an abundance of texture - is the quality expressed in the sketch of A SAGUARO CACTUS PLANT. The quantity of the *linework* shows the exact nature of the desert plant.

←

A uniformity of texture is expressed in the example of THE STACK OF BRICKS.

→

Profusion and quality of the hair are expressed by the distribution of coarse texture, over the face of THE SCOTTISH BULL.

→

The enormous number of individual blades forms A GRASS CLUSTER. The nature and amount of *linework* define the character of profusion inherent in the grass clusters.

For a flower, a ball, a bubble or a glass,
The gentle curve of an elegant brass;
Roughness or texture may mean a folly,
To draw a sketch, successfully.

To show elephant-grass or a bull in terror,
Down playing its roughness, is an error;
Ample of it, is certainly not a waste,
To draw a sketch - such is best.

JUDGING TEXTURE AGAINST THE BLANK AREAS

A proper balance between the textured and the plain areas, within the sketch, helps attain a desired look. The accentuated area, having texture, must be large enough to create an impact.

However, if the sketch is burdened with excessive *linework*, it looks confused and loses its vital balance. Therefore, only one or two areas should be chosen to add weight of concentrated *linework* to balance the remaining plain areas.

● **Germ of the idea**

An awareness of the relationship between the blank area and the texture, within the sketch, is required to obtain the desired balance.

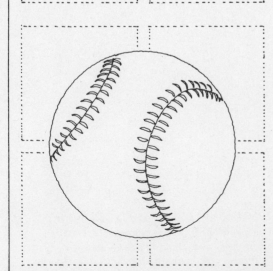

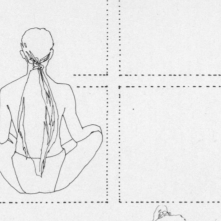

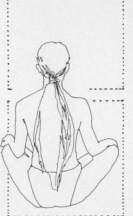

In the sketch of THE GROUP OF TREES, the two textured areas - one at the top and the other at the bottom - tie the sketch together. ↓

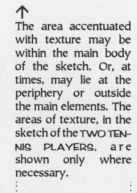

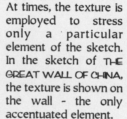

At times, the texture is employed to stress only a particular element of the sketch. In the sketch of THE GREAT WALL OF CHINA, the texture is shown on the wall - the only accentuated element.

In the sketch of A GIRL ON THE SWING, shown below, the chain supporting the swing is the element emphasized with texture. ↓

↑ The area accentuated with texture may be within the main body of the sketch. Or, at times, may lie at the periphery or outside the main elements. The areas of texture, in the sketch of the TWO TENNIS PLAYERS, are shown only where necessary.

← The eye wanders over the entire sketch of THE SOFT DRINK CANS, because the texture is uniformly spread.

→ The sketch of THE PINE CONES, even though contains a uniform texture overall, appears delicate. However, the eye is gradually attracted towards the small cone, as a result of comparatively more *linework* employed to show its rounded top.

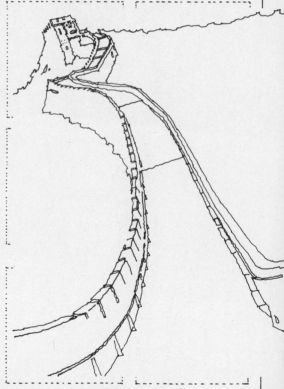

→ If the texture is spread all over, it may be difficult for the eye to comprehend the sketch quickly. In the sketch of A LION, it takes a moment before it is clearly recognized.

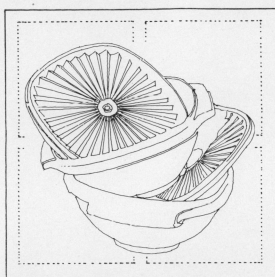

↑
The radiating corrugations on the plastic lids create a striking texture, as shown in the sketch of the common TUPPERWARE UTENSILS. The textured areas are so arranged that a

Notice the balance between the areas of concentrated texture on the shoes of THE BOY DRAWING A SKETCH and the remaining *linework* provided by the surrounding figure. The

good balance between the texture and the blank area is achieved.

The isolated stripes of texture add richness to the drawing of A FRESH GRADUATE.
↓

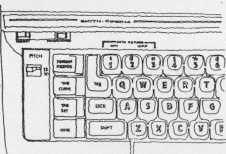

concentrated texture attracts more attention than the other elements.
↓

A quality of soft texture is achieved by avoiding concentration of *linework* in any particular area. The result

of this approach is shown in the sketch of THE KEYBOARD OF A TYPEWRITER.
↓

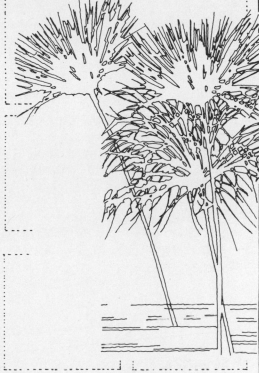

In the sketch of THE SKELETON OF A FISH, the profuse *linework*, necessary to explain the structure of the bones, does not burden the sketch.
↓

↑
In the sketch of THE POP SINGER, the textured area is larger than the plain area. A sketch burdened with excessive *linework* may, at times, lose its elegance.

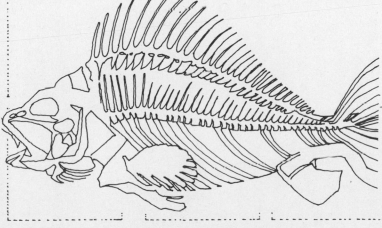

←
More than one type of texture may be quite appropriate in certain situations, as in the sketch of A CANADIAN PONY. Note that the texture used for showing the rope is different than the kind used for the mane of the pony.

↑
A concentration of *linework*, creating a dense texture, is located only in the upper part of the sketch of THE PAPYRUS PLANTS growing in the Nile Valley. The remaining area, though practically devoid of much *linework*, receives an interesting balance in the overall sketch.

Density of linework, forms the texture,
And the plain areas, balance the mixture;
The textured areas may only be one or two,
To create a desired effect, such will do .

KEY TO COMPOSITIONS

The specific placement of the elements within the sketch and the graphic positioning of the sketch itself within its frame, form the overall composition.

The composition - the organization of various elements of a sketch - falls in one of the following five types.

● **Symmetrical**

Bilaterally symmetrical compositions are the most common instances of this group. In this type of composition, a visual balance is achieved by creating a perfect symmetry along the central axis.

The sketches - of THE PITCHER, THE HANGING LIGHT FIXTURE and THE MOTIF OF THE WINGED RAMS - are examples of a composition having symmetry along the central vertical axis.

An idea of bilateral symmetry has been a fascination through the ages. Many historical buildings, which have achieved the quality of timelessness, are based on this very concept.

Symmetry gives an established look and, hence, has been traditionally used throughout the world.

↑ The adjoining sketch of THE TAJ MAHAL is an example of the symmetrical building design.

The minarets and the domes of the structure are so placed that the overall composition does not exhibit the monotony that is typically inherent in a composition of repetitive geometric shapes.

● **Asymmetrical**

The arrangement of elements, not perfectly symmetrical along the central axis, forms an asymmetrical composition.

The MAPLE LEAF shown above is basically symmetrical, but lacks a perfect symmetry along its central axis.

The sketch of A HAND shows its inherent imbalance in symmetry.

← A PINE TREE appears symmetrical in its form. However, a closer look - as the sketch shows - reveals the asymmetry in its shape.

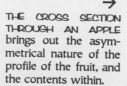

→ THE CROSS SECTION THROUGH AN APPLE brings out the asymmetrical nature of the profile of the fruit, and the contents within.

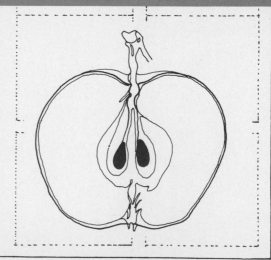

↑
In the sketch of AN ORNAMENTAL GATE, each half, with its intricate ornamentation and the supporting structure, is a mirror image of the other.

In nature, examples of bilateral symmetry are common, such as, A HOUSEFLY. A BUTTERFLY. A BIPINNATE LEAF OF *POINSETTIA REGIA* and A BEETLE.

↑ The sketch of AN ASSYRIAN MOTIF shows a symmetrical balance along its two axes - vertical and horizontal.

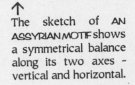

A sketch of THE DUCKS SWIMMING IN WATER, is an example of a typical composition having symmetry along the central horizontal axis.
↓

A picture of THE KING OF SPADES is also an example of a symmetrical balance. The symmetry in this case is obtained by rotating the design around its diagonal axis.
↓

↑ It is said that no two SNOW FLAKES have same shape. However, within themselves they are polysymmetrical.

← The sketch of THE ELEPHANTS shows a symmetrical theme but lacks exactness in symmetry. The same is true for the sketch of A GROUP OF FLAMINGOES →

THE FACE OF THE BOY, looked from front, shows that it is not quite symmetrical along its central axis. The slight variation of details makes the sketch asymmetric.

← In the sketch of THE CADUCEUS, it takes a moment to realize that the design is not symmetric along its central axis. The spiral twist in the pattern of snakes causes the asymmetry in balance.
→

The prestigious SEAL OF THE UNITED STATES OF AMERICA is an example of a beautiful asymmetric graphic design.

Directional

The arrangement of elements that invokes a sense of direction in the sketch, in relation to its frame, constitutes a directional composition. A diagonal composition is a common example of this category.

Sometimes, to create a specific effect, the elements of the sketch are placed to suggest a flow in more than one direction or to indicate a sudden change in the direction of their flow.

↑ The sketch of A THORNY BRANCH of an acacia shrub suggests a diagonal composition in a square frame.

→ The adjoining sketch of A MUSICIAN PLAYING HORN, shown in a rectangular frame, also produces a diagonal composition.

→ The sketch of a flamboyant JAPANESE ROOSTER perched on a wall, with the trail of its majestic tail, leads into a diagonal composition when set in a vertical rectangular frame.

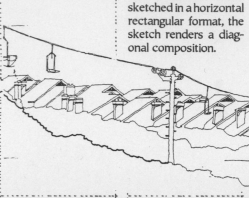

THE CABLE CARS running along a slope of the mountain when sketched in a horizontal rectangular format, the sketch renders a diagonal composition.

Shape-based

The overall arrangement of the elements of a sketch sometimes forms a configuration that can be roughly identified with a geometric shape. Such an arrangement constitutes a shape-based composition.

Typically, the formations, such as a triangular, square, rectangular, circular, L-shaped, etc., fall in this category.

→ In the sketch of THE BOY PLAYING FLUTE, the extended leg, the vertical masonry wall and the remaining empty space in the square frame, form an overall L-shaped composition.

As THE SPRINTING CHEETAH leaps forward using its hind legs, it momentarily takes support on the ground with one of his forelegs. At this moment, the profile of the animal forms a triangular composition. In this case, the configuration is an inverted triangle with its apex at the bottom.

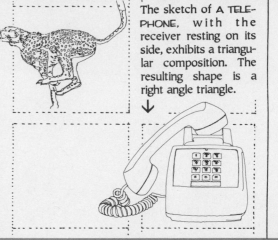

The sketch of A TELEPHONE, with the receiver resting on its side, exhibits a triangular composition. The resulting shape is a right angle triangle.

↓

Abstract

A composition that does not belong to any of the above types, falls in the abstract category.

The adjoining examples do not express any symmetry, flow of direction, or an overall geometric shape, and thus are abstract compositions.

The compositions, particularly of the symmetrical nature, follow rigid rules. Whereas, the abstract compositions, being spontaneous, do not follow set rules of formality. Indeed, such compositions are many times consciously designed to dissociate themselves from the generally identifiable forms and shapes. It is interesting to note that an abstract composition also can be well-balanced.

→ The sketch of THE BRANCH OF A TREE shown here, has similar composition as the abstract sketch shown on the left. The difference is that this sketch is designed to portray an identifiable object.

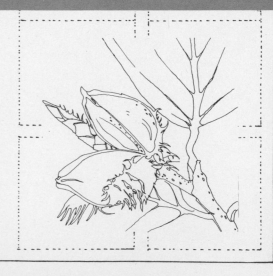

The adjoining sketch of THE SET OF FLAME-TORCHES produces a definite directional composition, though not quite diagonal.

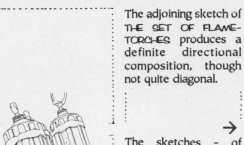

The sketches - of MAHATMA GANDHI and a detail from THE MUHAMMAD ALI MOSQUE, Cairo - drawn in a suitable frame, suggest a vertical composition.

→

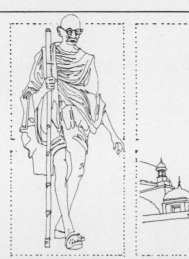

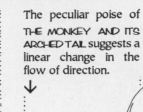

The peculiar poise of THE MONKEY AND ITS ARCHED TAIL suggests a linear change in the flow of direction.

↓

The sketch of THE SWIMMING SHARKS indicates a sudden change in the direction of flow.

↓

The sketch of A BRANCH OF MICHELIA CHAMPACA has a square composition in a square frame. The sketch of AN ENTABLATURE WITH THE IONIC CAPITAL is a vertical rectangular composition. THE PAIR OF BULLS shows a rectangular composition in a square frame. The sketch of THE ORANGES shows a horizontal rectangular composition.

→

The sketch of A WINDING SNAKE has a circular composition in a square frame.

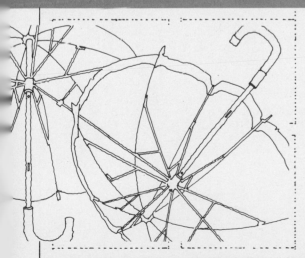

←

The sketch of THE OPEN UMBRELLAS is basically a diagonal theme in a rectangular format. But, its directional flow is disturbed by the protruding handles, leading in an abstract form.

→

The sketch of the TWO BOYS SITTING ON A WALL, is neither a directional nor a shape-based theme.

Though each of THE THORNY FRUITS is spherical in shape, their random placement in the sketch leads to an abstract composition.

→

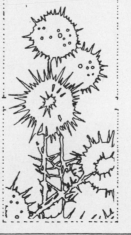

In a circle is seen, the perfect symmetry,
In a pine tree, an asymmetry;
Some layouts suggest a directional theme,
Based on a shape, a few may seem;
The remaining ones, with no rule, in fact,
Are classified as - the compositions abstract.

LEVEL OF MOTION

Often, the objects drawn in a sketch suggest a degree of motion, ranging from the static state to a dynamic state.

↑ The sketch of THE GARBAGE BAGS placed on the sidewalk reflects their inherent stationary nature.

THE HIGHWAY NETWORK, though static in its nature, suggests movement due to its snake-like shape.

↓

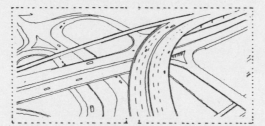

THE SALE SIGN hanging from its post, THE BIRD parched on a wall, and THE BOY holding the soccer ball, indicate no degree of movement.

PAINTING FOR SALE
Creative Group 2
881 8712

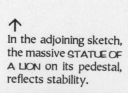

↑ In the adjoining sketch, the massive STATUE OF A LION on its pedestal, reflects stability.

189

→ THE ANCHORED BOAT, floating on water, reflects a gentle sway of movement.

The sketches of THE LADY pulling a baby buggy. THE BOY playing baseball. THE BUCKET being pulled up from the well, and THE DUCKS swimming in water, indicate a gentle movement.

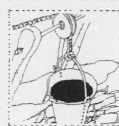

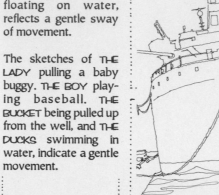

↑ In the adjoining sketch, the action of THE MAN PUSHING A CART, suggests a certain degree of motion.

The sketches of THE GIRL ON A HIGH SWING and THE BABY SITTING IN A SWING, reflect a good degree of motion.

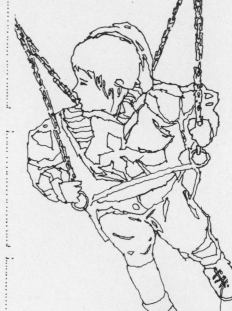

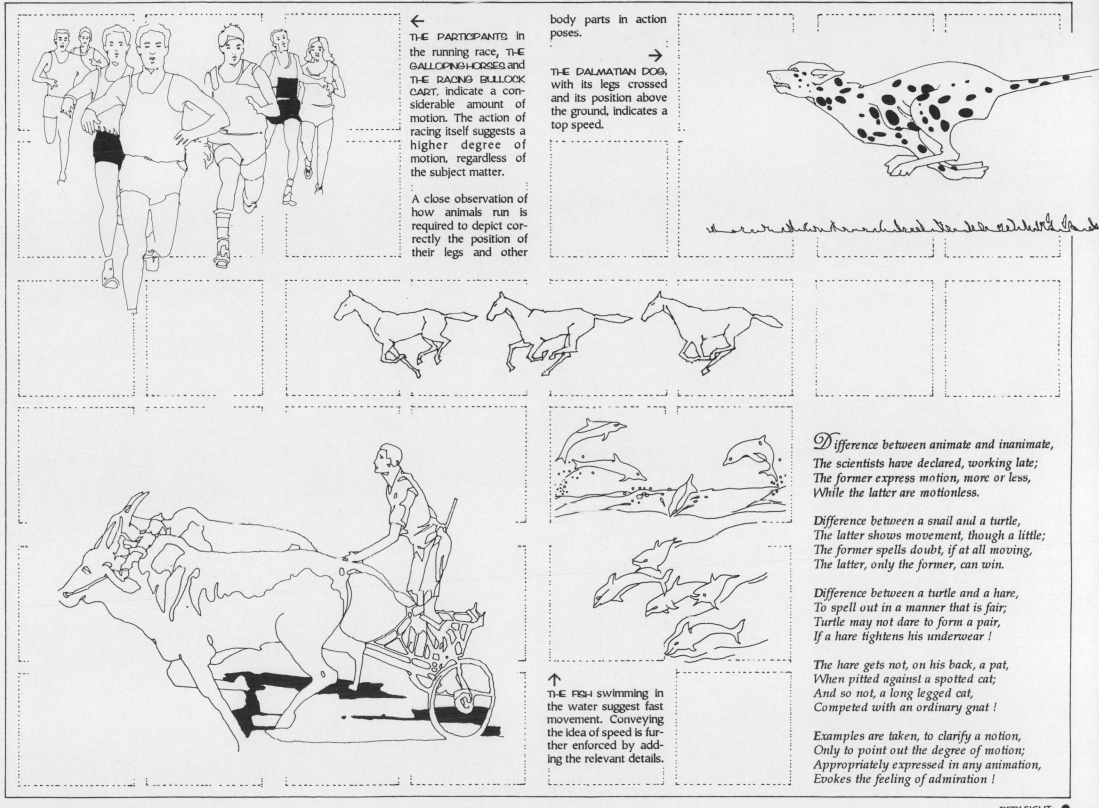

← THE PARTICIPANTS in the running race, THE GALLOPING HORSES and THE RACING BULLOCK CART, indicate a considerable amount of motion. The action of racing itself suggests a higher degree of motion, regardless of the subject matter.

A close observation of how animals run is required to depict correctly the position of their legs and other body parts in action poses.

→ THE DALMATIAN DOG, with its legs crossed and its position above the ground, indicates a top speed.

↑ THE FISH swimming in the water suggest fast movement. Conveying the idea of speed is further enforced by adding the relevant details.

Difference between animate and inanimate,
The scientists have declared, working late;
The former express motion, more or less,
While the latter are motionless.

Difference between a snail and a turtle,
The latter shows movement, though a little;
The former spells doubt, if at all moving,
The latter, only the former, can win.

Difference between a turtle and a hare,
To spell out in a manner that is fair;
Turtle may not dare to form a pair,
If a hare tightens his underwear !

The hare gets not, on his back, a pat,
When pitted against a spotted cat;
And so not, a long legged cat,
Competed with an ordinary gnat !

Examples are taken, to clarify a notion,
Only to point out the degree of motion;
Appropriately expressed in any animation,
Evokes the feeling of admiration !

MAKE-UP OF THE OBJECTS

The knowledge of the actual make-up of an object is necessary to draw its sketch correctly.

The following example illustrates, how A TIMBER LAMPPOST is typically mounted on the concrete base along the sidewalks, in Canada.

Step 1 shows a round wooden pole, with a flat base, placed on a previously built rectangular concrete pad.

Step 2 shows the position of the two prefabricated metal brackets. Each bracket is L-shaped, with sloping side walls. Its shorter arm rests on the concrete pad, so that the metal bolts, previously mounted in the concrete pad, come out through its holes. The longer arm butts against the wooden post. The brackets are placed on each side of the post, on the concrete base, as shown.

Step 3 shows the curved shaped metal anchors with threaded ends to receive the nuts. Four such anchors are used, two on each side of the brackets.

Step 4 shows the placement of nuts on the metal anchors.

The correctness of the sketch of the lamppost, like any other object, depends upon the clear understanding of how its various elements are put together.

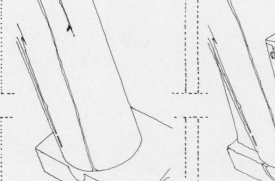

The sketch of THE BARBED WIRE shows, how a set of two barbs is mounted on the twisted pair of wires. The two short pieces of wire are diagonally cut into sharp points and are intertwined to form the barbs. For the purpose of understanding, one barb in each pair is shown in solid tone.

In order to draw the sketch of A GRAFTED PLANT, it is desirable to know the steps involved in grafting.

The adjoining sketch shows the three basic steps involved - First, preparing the branches for a graft, secondly, positioning the branches together and tying them and finally, pruning the grafts.

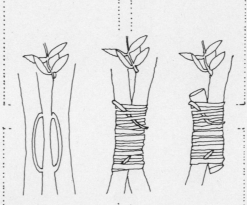

A simple weave of A BAMBOO BASKET is explained in the adjoining figure. Because the construction of the weave is shown correctly, the object is easily identified.

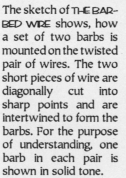

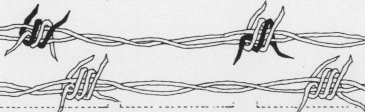

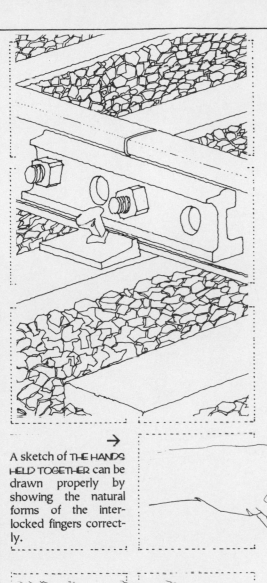

The sketch shows a typical connection of a steel rail of A RAILWAY TRACK. The timber railroad-ties, a fishplate, the nuts, the bolts, etc., are shown in their right places.

The sketch of A PAIR OF RUNNING SHOES looks natural if their make-up and the method of tying laces, is shown properly.

In the examples - of A SPIKE OF AEGILOPS SPELT shown above and THE EAR OF TRITICUM SATIVUM shown on the right - each kernel is held in its place in the jacket of its skin. Not until one knows the exact fashion in which they are arranged on the wavy central shaft, one can properly draw their sketches.

The sketch of A FLY-ING BAT shows its front and rear legs, skin flap, extended phalanges and claws. It explains the structure of the mammal.

A sketch of THE HANDS HELD TOGETHER can be drawn properly by showing the natural forms of the inter-locked fingers correct-ly.

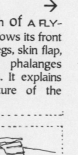

The sketch shows THE SHADOW OF A DRIED TREE, cast on concrete steps. It explains how a shadow pattern is formed on different planes along the risers and the treads of the steps.

A set of THE INDIAN DRUMS is an interesting object to draw, once its make-up is properly understood.

Attempted once, then twice, then the third time,
Failed drawing a simple sketch, every single time;
Wondered why, what went wrong, where was the folly ?
At the end, determined then, to think logically.

To have no frustrations, further,
And to face the fears, worst;
How the object is put together,
Must be understood first !

NATURE OF PATTERNS

An expression of a repetitive element within the sketch, is the basic concept of pattern.

A casual distribution of similar objects is seen in the adjoining three examples, namely THE STRIPED GAS BALLOONS flying in the sky, the well-proportioned WATER PITCHERS and the decorative wings of THE BUTTERFLIES resting on a vine. A repetition of the units is obvious in each case.

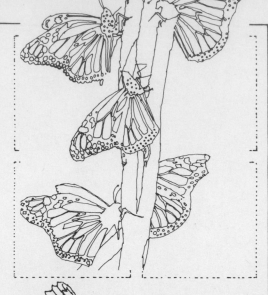

↑
THE HONEYBEES in a swarm or THE PALM TREES in a group, when sketched, can render interesting irregular patterns. The sketch of the palm trees shows that the elements need

not be of same size to form a pattern, as long as they have a similar shape.

Learning from nature, man has employed the idea of the pattern for his creativity. The sketches of A WIRE MESH of a fence and A MARBLE GRILL of a window show two examples of regular patterns. In these cases, a particular geometric shape is repeated many times to create each pattern.

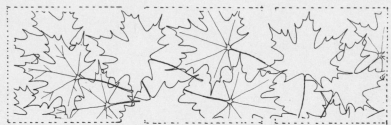

←
The circular arrangement of the feathers in A SHUTTLECOCK creates an interesting pattern.

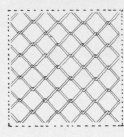

● Germ of the idea

The organic arrangement of the hexagonal cells in a honeycomb is one of the most common ideas of patterns found in the nature.

A cluster of MAPLE LEAVES, a group of TRILLIUM FLOWERS and a number of sword-like HORNS OF THE ANTELOPES, form interesting patterns as seen in nature.

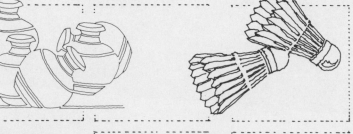

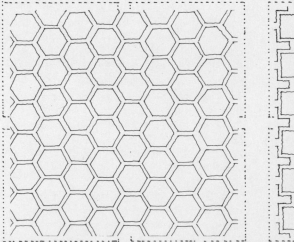

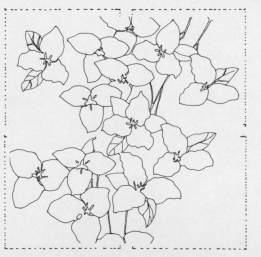

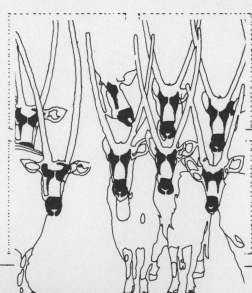

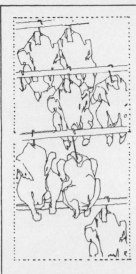

The interesting patterns can be visualized in the incidental man-made arrangements of various objects, as seen in the sketch of THE CHICKEN BREASTS displayed in the meat market.

→

The patterns on THE CLOTHING OF PEOPLE are a common sight. Such patterns are numerous, limited only to the imagination of the garment designers.

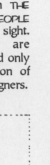

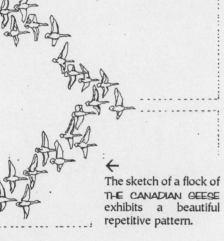

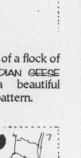

The sketch of a flock of THE CANADIAN GEESE exhibits a beautiful repetitive pattern.

Repetition of a standard module, arranged consciously or unconsciously, creates a visual pattern. THE STACK OF BRICKS forms an orderly pattern of rectangles and circles. The pattern of A STONE RAILING is formed out of a series of identical balusters. The structural steel members of AN ELECTRICAL PYLON exhibit a repetitive geometric pattern.

↓

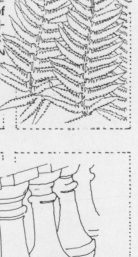

←

The adjoining sketch of the pinnate FRONDS OF A FERN shows the repetitive pattern of a typical leaflet.

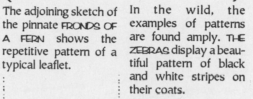

→

In the wild, the examples of patterns are found amply. THE ZEBRAS display a beautiful pattern of black and white stripes on their coats.

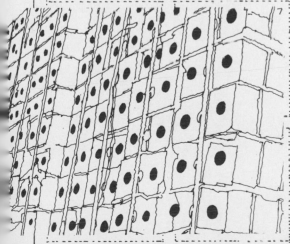

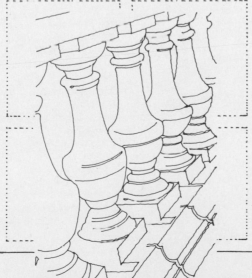

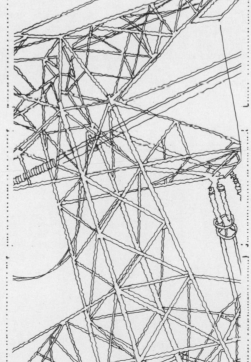

Just a single object on its own,
Did not quite sing;
Repeated a few times, however,
Looked more interesting.

The idea is seen, in the house of bees,
So also, in a group of palm trees;
Noticed the same, in the flying geese,
And again, in a cluster of maple leaves.

Repetition of elements, a key to govern,
Shows explicitly, a leaf of fern;
In nature everywhere, this lesson we learn,
Such is the concept behind a pattern.

On FOCUS OF INTEREST

Sometimes, a point of interest is specifically created in a sketch, in order to attract the attention. In such a theme, the sketch is designed so that the eye does not wander all over, but, is channelled to rest on the key part of the sketch. The key element can be highlighted by using different ideas.

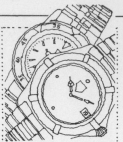

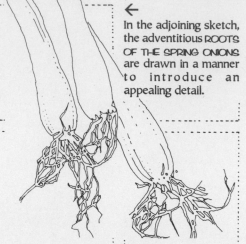

The plain faces of THE WRIST WATCHES are accentuated by the adjoining texture of the watch bands.

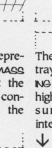

↑ The blank areas representing THE LAND MASS stand out against the surrounding soft contrast created by the lines of reference.

The sunlit area, portraying THE BOY WAVING HAND, creates a high contrast with the surrounding dark interior.
↓

← In the adjoining sketch, the adventitious ROOTS OF THE SPRING ONIONS are drawn in a manner to introduce an appealing detail.

In the sketch of A BOY TAKING PICTURE, the detail information on the front section of the camera holds attention.

THE MAN LOOKING AT THE CAT and the cat in turn staring at the ball of wool, channel the viewer's attention to the ball. The same is true in the sketch of THE CAT WATCHING ITS OWN REFLECTION in the mirror.

← Almost perfectly round shape of THE BERRIES on a branch attracts attention.

Reversing only one word, from the sign of AN ADVERTISEMENT, induces the reader to pause and read it more than once. A plain SALE SIGN, in contrast with the surrounding elements of texture, stands out as a focus of interest.

← The reflections on the eyeballs of THE CAT establish an eye-contact with the viewer, and become the focus in the sketch.

A single patch of dark tone, regardless of its size, is the key element in the sketch of THE VILLAGERS entertaining themselves.
↓

An introduction of the solid tone in the sketch of A PEACOCK FEATHER, creates a focus of attention. →

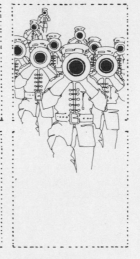

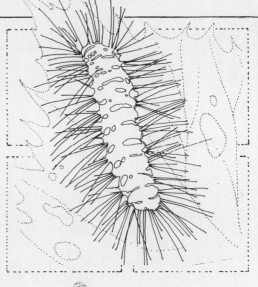

← In the sketch of the plain looking KITCHEN UTENSILS, the patch of holes on the strainer attracts attention. The small textured area causes a contrast against the smooth surfaces of the pots.

Round areas of the bugles are the points of attraction in the above sketch. In the sketch on the right, circular shape of the wheel, along with its placement in the foreground, acts as a focus of attention.

In nature, we find many animals having innate striking features. The hairy texture in the sketch of THE CATER-PILLAR, and the dark spots in the sketch of THE CHEETAH, add impact to the sketches.

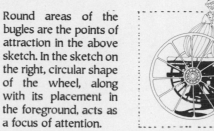

The dark black alphabets on the tiles highlight the sketch of THE GAME OF SCRABBLE. The striking dark stripes representing THE PIANO KEYS act as a key element that attracts attention.

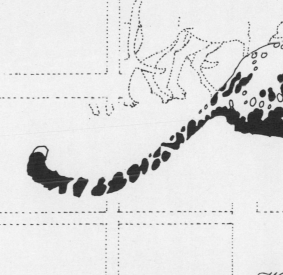

Why are we attracted to particular things,
Specific aspects, ideas, and some drawings ?
They hold our eye, for seconds and a fraction,
Arresting attention with, focus of attraction.

PROVIDING A SUSPENSE

An idea of suspense is introduced in a theme by deliberately deleting or obscuring a part of the sketch. However, a suggestion of the completeness of the theme is clearly evident.

The sketch is designed in such a way that, though it is drawn only partially, it is easy for the viewer to imagine its completeness without much difficulty. The concept stimulates the creative faculty of mind.

● **Germ of the idea**

A blank canvass framed and hung in a museum would generate a great degree of suspense in the minds of the viewers, to search for something in it.

In the adjoining sketch of THE GIRL PEEPING OVER THE WALL, much of her body is hidden behind the wall. An unexpected sudden break in the continuity of the girl's profile, caused by the line representing the top edge of the wall, creates suspense. The same is true with the sketch of THE MAN READING THE NEWSPAPER.

→ In the adjoining sketch, the eyes of THE MAN AND THE CHILD, being hidden behind the metal bars, cause a sense of incompleteness in the sketch. Because of the absence of the eye contact, the intimacy is not established and relating to the sketch becomes difficult.

In the adjoining sketch, the faces of A MAN AND A WOMAN SITTING IN THE CHAIRS. are hidden behind the sides of the chairs. Even though an eye contact is not possible with the people shown, the sketch can be visualized fully with imagination. In this case, the mind is made to ponder for a second, before the subject matter is properly understood. ↓

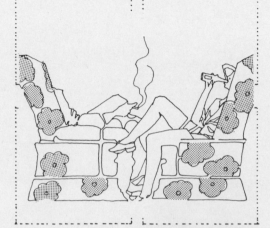

Only a partial depiction of the design of THE SYMMETRICAL VASE is enough for the eye to complete it. Similar idea is true in the sketch of THE BUDDHA.

In some cases, only a striking feature of an object is drawn to represent it. In the sketch of THE KILLER WHALES swimming in the ocean, the tiny fins protruding through the surface of water, is the indication of the mystery beneath them. They are enough to represent the complete idea of the enormous bodies, underneath. The same idea is suggested in the sketch of THE GROUP OF DOLPHINS. In this case, the elements under the water surface are partially visible as a result of their proximity to the viewer.

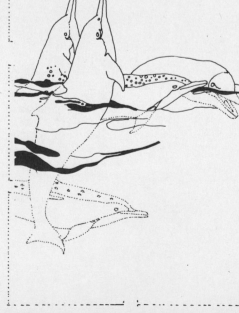

In the sketch of THE SINGER ON A STAGE, wearing a dark dress, the spot-lights highlight her figure, other than a part of her right arm. Only her right palm, under the spotlight, is visible; while the rest of her arm, covered with the sleeve, is not visible amid the dark back-ground.

The same idea is conveyed in the sketch of THE GIRL IN A DARK GOWN. The position of her crossed arms is obvious, simply from the profiles of the hands.

An interesting example of an incomplete sketch conveying the full sense of its completeness, is seen in the case of the adjoining figure of THE SOFT DRINK BOTTLES. Here, the profile of the transparent glass is not shown. However, the labels and the lids, placed apart from each other, suggest the full picture of the objects.

The sketch below shows THE INDIAN WATER BUFFALOS cooling themselves off in shallow water ponds. The buffalos like to stay afloat for a long time, keeping their heads above water. As the animals float, sometimes their backs remain above water, partially. The heads and the backs, being visible above water, have a visual discontinuity, as the viewer perceives them.

At times, in a larger group, it is difficult to identify all the buffalos, with their heads and the corresponding backs.

In some instances, confusion is deliberately created, making a viewer search and identify the various elements of the sketch. The theme is portrayed in the sketch of THE THREE BOYS PLAYING.

In the sketch of THE HERD OF GIRAFFES, the patterns on their coats are intermixed, causing confusion in identifying them clearly.

In the sketch of A TIGER STANDING IN THE TALL GRASS, the stripes on his body blend so well with the adjoining grass blades that a clear identification of the animal is puzzling.

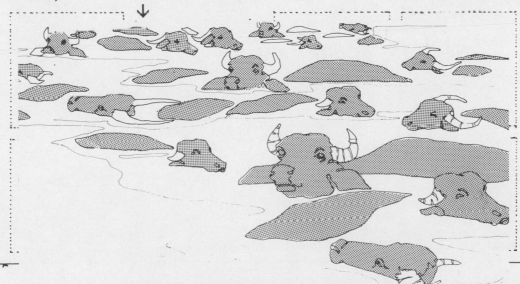

One fine morning, for the pleasure's sake,
I visited my farm and the nearby lake;
The floating dark patches on the cool water,
Created the suspense - what's the matter ?

It was hard to figure out, the head or tail,
Or, was it a head or a tail ?
I took my stance, had a closer glance,
Two dark patches rose above, by chance.

They joined into one, the head and the tail,
As, a water buffalo came up, without fail;
The secret known - the head and backbone,
Appeared disjointed by water alone !

Q UEST FOR UNIQUE IDEAS

Some sketches look more attractive than others due to a special idea embodied in them. It may relate to a unique pose, an unusual angle of viewing, an extraordinary concept or the like. They contain a definite theme that holds the attention of the viewer.

● **Germ of the idea**

A blank canvas, framed and hung in an art gallery, would be considered quite unusual for itself to be considered as an artwork, since it defies the conventional notion of a work of art.

← The sketch of THE GIRL READING A BOOK portrays an unusual pose. It takes an effort to analyze the posture. The unusual angle of viewing makes it so.

→ The funny shape of THE FLYING FLAMINGOS, with their dark tipped wings against the clear background of the sky, makes an unusually interesting sketch.

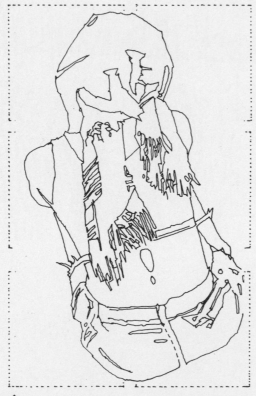

↑ The simple pose of THE GIRL SITTING ON GROUND, though her face is not visible, is an interesting and unusual subject matter for a sketch. The lace of the towel on her head,

helps add an interesting detail to this simple sketch.

→ The sketch of THE GIRL TAKING EXERCISE, expressing the stress, is simple but appealing.

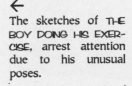

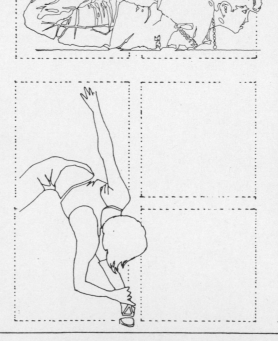

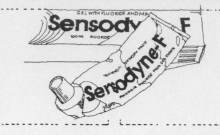

↑ A TOOTHPASTE in its twisted form, is a commonplace. However, if sketched, it results into a novelty.

← The sketches of THE BOY DOING HIS EXERCISE, arrest attention due to his unusual poses.

THE SHADOW PATTERN, of the fence cast on the undulated ground surface and on the tree trunk, creates an unusual graphic effect. ↓

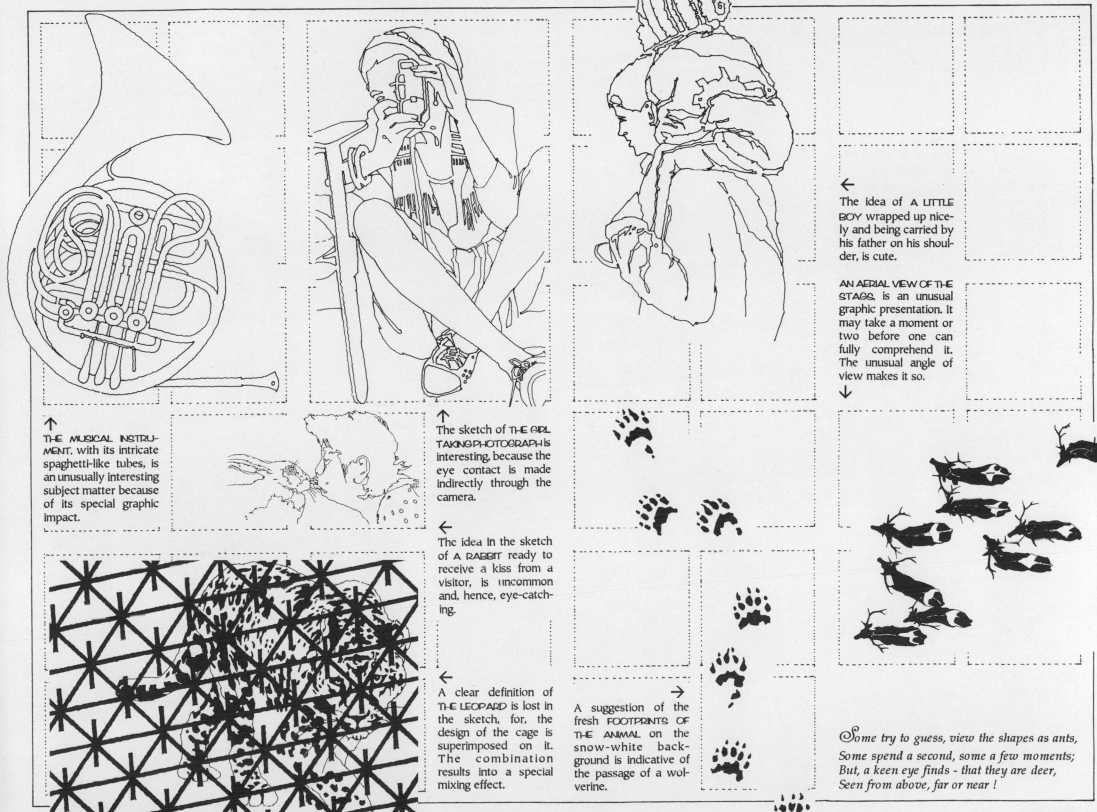

↑ THE MUSICAL INSTRUMENT, with its intricate spaghetti-like tubes, is an unusually interesting subject matter because of its special graphic impact.

The sketch of THE GIRL TAKING PHOTOGRAPH is interesting, because the eye contact is made indirectly through the camera.

← The idea in the sketch of A RABBIT ready to receive a kiss from a visitor, is uncommon and, hence, eye-catching.

← The idea of A LITTLE BOY wrapped up nicely and being carried by his father on his shoulder, is cute.

AN AERIAL VIEW OF THE STAGS, is an unusual graphic presentation. It may take a moment or two before one can fully comprehend it. The unusual angle of view makes it so. ↓

← A clear definition of THE LEOPARD is lost in the sketch, for, the design of the cage is superimposed on it. The combination results into a special mixing effect.

→ A suggestion of the fresh FOOTPRINTS OF THE ANIMAL on the snow-white background is indicative of the passage of a wolverine.

𝒮ome try to guess, view the shapes as ants,
Some spend a second, some a few moments;
But, a keen eye finds - that they are deer,
Seen from above, far or near !

RANDOM DISTRIBUTION OF SOLID TONES

Sometimes, the areas of solid tone are randomly distributed in the sketch, in order to create movement of the eye over the entire sketch.

The arbitrary placement of the solid tone imparts an abstract character to the sketch.

● **Germ of the idea**

A pattern produced by an accidental spill of ink, has all the features of a random distribution of solid tones.

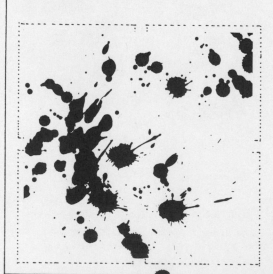

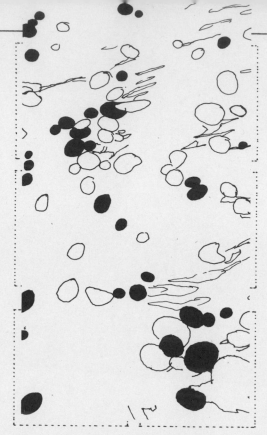

The sketch of an uneven distribution of coloured PEBBLES ON A BEACH, is an extension of the basic concept.

→ The adjoining example of THE FIREWORKS, shows a random distribution of white tone on the black background.

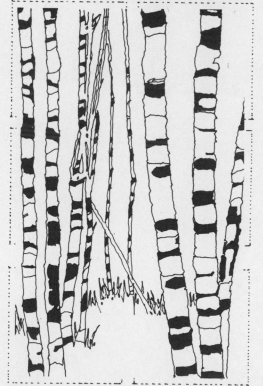

← In the sketch of THE DRUMS supported on tripods, the circular black spots display the effect of sporadic placement of dark areas.

↑ The dark patches scattered on THE TRUNKS OF THE ASPEN TREES, create an overall abstract pattern.

← The black heads of THE BIRDS create a random distribution of dark shapes in the adjoining sketch.

← In the adjoining sketches, the dark colour of THE GOATS and a casual arrangement of the black pieces on THE CHESS BOARD, create the effects of random distribution of solid tones.

↓

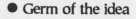

The uneven placement of the dark areas - representing the lettering in the sketch of THE COKE CANS, the black suite of THE PLAYING CARDS and the round clappers of THE HANGING BELLS - convey the idea of random distribution of solid tones.

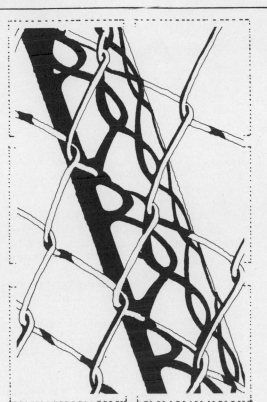

An individual PENGUIN symbolizes a large white patch on a dark background, or, a dark patch on a white background. However, when in an assembly, the dark patches on these birds form a wonderful abstract pattern - against the white patches and the surrounding white of the snow.
↓

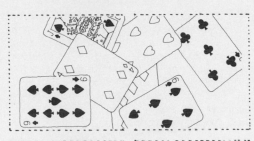

↑
The dark coloured PODS HANGING FROM THE ACACIA TREE provide a striking example of the random distribution of solid tone. We often witness such simple but interesting effects everywhere. However, for our minds

to register them that way, it takes training of the eye and a keen observation.

Here, the dark tones are in the form of thin but bold lines represent the legs of THE FLAMINGOS.
↓

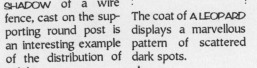

↑
THE IRREGULAR SHADOW of a wire fence, cast on the supporting round post is an interesting example of the distribution of solid tone.

The coat of A LEOPARD displays a marvellous pattern of scattered dark spots.
↓

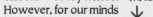

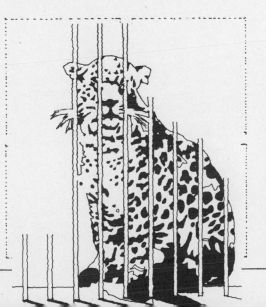

Wearing their coats perfectly tight,
White on black or black on white;
Without an ado, without a fight,
All joined together, in the moonlit night.

Scattered here and there, they stood upright,
Ignoring the arrangement - wrong or right;
The family of penguins, on the snow-white,
Produced quite a fascinating sight !

SETTING UP THE CONTRAST

In order to provide a dynamic expression to each element of the work of art, the black and white tonal areas are arranged in juxtaposition, conducive to intensifying the tonal values of the elements. This sets up a contrast between the two tones.

A high contrast is normally created to add an impact to the sketch. It could be achieved by using a texture or a solid tone.

● **Germ of the idea**

A comparatively smaller area of the black tone against its larger white background, or vice versa, sets up a strong contrast, attracting attention.

↑
Here, due to the white background provided by the paper, the contrasting colour of THE BLACK HORSE stands out prominently and attracts attention. Whereas, the white

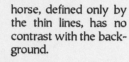

A dark pattern on THE DOG stands out because of the contrast with its light background.
↓

horse, defined only by the thin lines, has no contrast with the background.

In the adjoining two sketches of THE CHILDREN, the juxtaposition of the black and white tones produces a good balance between the tones. In one sketch the black and white tones are intermixed; whereas in the other, the tones are placed next to each other.

→
In the sketch of A CAMEL AND THE RIDERS, the dark shadow of the camel is specifically shown to depict the typical brightness of the tropical sun in the Egyptian desert. The decorative dark design on the apron, ties well the figures of the camel and the riders. The black and the white tones are intermixed to create a balance in the sketch.

↑
In the adjoining sketch, the profile of A TEMPLE is seen through a window screen. The brightness of the exterior is depicted properly by showing the contrasting dark-ness of the interior space. Because of the high contrast, the eye registers the dark pattern of the screen first, before the attention goes to the temple beyond.

↑
A softer contrast is achieved by using a grey tone, instead of a solid black, in the adjoining example.

The sketch shows the light coloured PIGEONS in the pigeonholes. The dark background highlights the pigeons. As the shadows of the birds are not shown, the sketch has a two-dimensional quality.
↓

↑
The sketch shows A WINDOW OF A HISTORIC BUILDING, in Canada. The dark tone representing the interior space creates an accent in the overall sketch. The contrast is maintained in spite of the texture produced by the *linework* on the exterior walls.

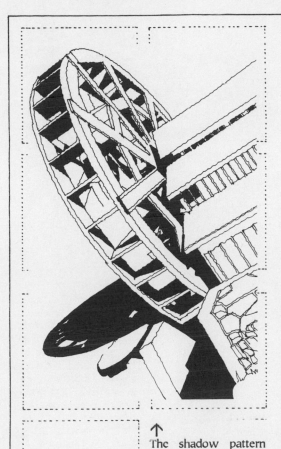

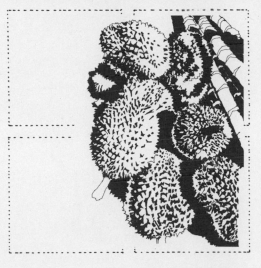

← The sketch of THE JACKFRUIT contains a mixture of the dark areas representing the fine bristles on the surface of the fruits and the solid black area showing the shadow of the fruits. The varying intensity of the tone, depicting the echinate character, gives a three-dimensional appearance to the fruit. The bristles also help properly depict the rough nature of the surface of the jackfruit.

↑ The sketch shows a part of THE ORNAMENTAL ARCHWAY over an entrance to a historical building. A clear definition of the fine stonework is achieved by establishing a local contrast, created by their shadows.

The idea of fine *linework* mixed with areas of high contrast is shown in the adjoining example of THE CHINESE CUTLERY. →

As the area of the dark tone becomes larger than the area of the white tone, the former becomes the background against which the latter stands out. The adjoining sketch shows A SUNLIT COURTYARD, as seen through an archway of the interior space of a historic building. Notice that, the intense brightness of the sun over the court yard is aptly portrayed by the contrasting darkness of the interior space that surrounds it.
←

As the outline is filled in fully with a solid tone, the object is recognized with its profile only. The silhouette-like expression is evident in the sketches of THE WASPS and THE BRANCH OF A TREE.

↑ The shadow pattern cast by various elements of A WATER MILL suggests the direction of sunlight. The contrast created by its shadow pattern helps define the elements of the water mill.

Notice the patchwork-like effect of the dark and the lit areas in the adjoining sketch. It is a result of bright sunlight falling on an uneven surface of the trunks of THE WHITE BIRCH TREES and their immediate surrounding. →

Similarly, the appropriate shadow pattern defines the profiles and contours of the body, in the sketch of MARY AND THE CHRIST.

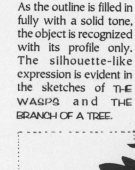

In the adjoining sketch, THE MOON AND THE STARS can be spotted unmistakably, against their very large background. →

For any sketch, in any case,
To catch the attention fast;
Tonal differences are juxtaposed,
To create a suitable contrast.

THE TECHNIQUE OF REVERSE EFFECT

Sometimes a special effect is injected in the sketch by showing certain parts of the elements in a tone, reverse to its background. The effect creates contrasts in sporadic areas, and alerts the eye to read the sketch more closely.

● Germ of the idea

In the illustration below, it is puzzling to the viewer to decide whether the black squares have a white background, or the other way around.

↑
In the adjoining sketch of A TILE PATTERN having white and black squares, set within each other, the reverse effect is evident in a simple form.

→
An interesting reverse effect is displayed in the sketch of THE GRASS against its background. As the background changes from white to black, it is difficult for a viewer to pinpoint the transition.

↑
Looking with squinted eyes, the adjoining sketch appears as an abstract pattern of black and white shapes. However, on a closer look, THE HERD OF BULLS becomes recognizable.

→
The lettering on THE POSTER depicting a proverb, is tricky to read as a result of the reverse effect. The effect generates a curiosity in the viewer's mind to read the poster.

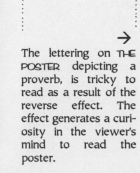

a friend in need is a friend indeed.

→
In the adjoining sketch, THE VOLLEYBALL NET is accentuated by showing it in the colour opposite to its background. The solid tone introduced to create the reverse effect adds a punch to the sketch as well as it helps tie various elements of the sketch together.

All the THREE LAMBS in the adjoining artwork are similar looking, however, the effect caused due to the reversing of their colour is quite interesting.

The candles, placed in their traditional CLAY CANDLE-HOLDERS, highlight the decorative elements on the latter. An appealing reverse effect is created because of the light and dark areas of the perforations on the pots.

In the adjoining sketch, a collage-effect is created, using THE CHESS-BOARD and the chessmen. The pieces assume a colour opposite to their backgrounds, and produce a mysteriously complex pattern.

In the sketch of THE PAIR OF ZEBRAS, it is not easy to conclude whether the animals have white stripes on a black coat or black stripes on a white coat. The reverse effect is a gift of nature to these beautiful animals.

The shadow of THE BULLOCK CART stands out in prominence against its bright background. In turn, the brightness of the wheel in the foreground, stands out against its own dark background.

The bullock sitting near the cart, without any striking features of its own, stands out due to the contrasting background of the dark shadows behind.

Between two nights, a day,
Or, between two days, a night;
Even the wise and learned say,
It is not easy to be right.

The candles emit light,
The light creates shadows;
The same shapes portray,
The light and the shadows.

Understanding the Residual Spaces

At times, the area enveloped between the elements of the sketch results into a form leading to a totally different sketch in itself.

It takes a keen eye and an effort to relate such enclosed space as a profile of an identifiable object.

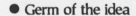
● Germ of the idea

In the adjoining sketch, the circular shapes are dominating. However, the residual area between them has a totally different shape - the shape of a diamond.

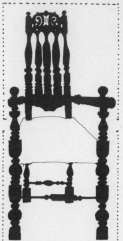

↑
The sketch shows a silhouette of A DECORATIVE WOODEN CHAIR. Notice the design of its back. The white areas between the vertical supports reflect the shapes of KNIVES AND SPOONS, the totally different objects in relation to the chair.

→
The dark figures - of A BOY AND A GIRL DANCING - have enclosed between them, a white area having a shape of A STANDING BEAR.

In the sketch of A MAN TALKING TO A BOY, the residual area takes the shape of A MAN IN A TOPCOAT.

The sketch of THE DANCING GIRLS, with a decorative pattern in the background, shows the residual area having a profile of THE SOUTH AMERICAN CONTINENT.

45

←
In the sketch of A MAN TALKING TO A BOY, the residual area takes the shape of A MAN IN A TOPCOAT.

In the sketch of THE THREE BOYS, the enclosed area takes the form of A SITTING ANIMAL.
↓

In the drawing of A MAN AND A WOMAN in the garden, the residual area between them has a shape of THE WHITE KNIGHT in the game of Chess.
↓

At times, a totally different object is concealed within the body of the main sketch. A careful observation reveals the identity of the hidden object.

→

In the adjoining sketch of A MODEL WEARING MINK, a closer look shows the hidden figure of A CHEETAH

Some sketches are so designed that they take a totally different meaning when the picture frame is turned around.

→

The adjoining sketch of A NINJA with the quiver on his back, becomes a sketch of THE HEAD OF A COW, when turned around at right angle.

→

The sketch of the THREE MONKEYS playing together - when turned upside down - becomes a sketch of A DACHSHUND.

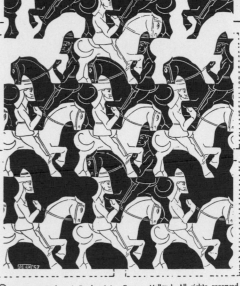

Reproduced here is a part of a classical sketch from the works of the Dutch artist, Mr. M. C. Escher. The sketch portrays A HORSE RIDER repeated a number of times, in order to create a pattern. The figure of the rider and the method of repetition is so designed that the areas between the figures also form the same theme, but in opposite direction and reverse tone.

Similarly, the drawing of the TWO YOUNG BIRDS sitting in their nest with their mouths open, becomes a sketch of A PAIR OF REINDEER.

In a regular pattern, is something hidden,
Of equal circles, with gaps forbidden ?
A casual glance reveals, within a second,
The residual space, having shape of diamond.

←

The adjoining drawing shows the profile of A SWIMMING DUCK. When the same sketch is completed by drawing its reflection in water, and then turned around at a right angle, a sketch of A WILDE-BEEST is the result !

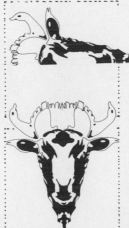

←

Similarly, in the adjoining sketch, the profile of TWO DUCKS - a white and a black - turns into a sketch of A BISON.

Similarly . . .
In an army of white horsemen, Escher found,
Something was hidden, he looked all around;
Concealed were the spies, of bad omen,
The opposing army of the black horsemen !

Likewise . . .
Negative space of an abstract pattern,
Can be identified and named rightly, in turn;
Such is the beauty of residual spaces,
Found amply, in many cases.

And hence . . .
To recognize the shape, of a residual space,
Of any image, in any case;
Needs no qualification, no degree holder,
'Cause, beauty lies in the eyes of beholder !

VARYING THE EMPHASIS

The appearance of a sketch depends on how its various elements are emphasized. The following illustrations show, how a distinctly different expression is given to a sketch, by applying a different technique each time.

A girl playing music

1. A minimum amount of *linework* is used to draw the figure of A GIRL PLAYING MUSIC. 2. The figure of the girl is emphasised against its background, by using thick lines to draw its profile. 3. Only selected areas of the figure are highlighted by applying a solid tone. 4. The figure of the girl is highlighted by creating a contrasting dark background.

A bunch of corn ears

1. An elegant look to the sketch of the corns is obtained with the use of a uniform *linework*. 2. Another dimension is added to the sketch by drawing some of the shucks with a heavier line. 3. A stronger visual impact is added by sporadically distributing the black tone, indicating the dark seeds. 4. A three-dimensional effect is obtained by drawing the cobs as secondary elements and accentuating the contrast on shucks by showing their deep shadows.

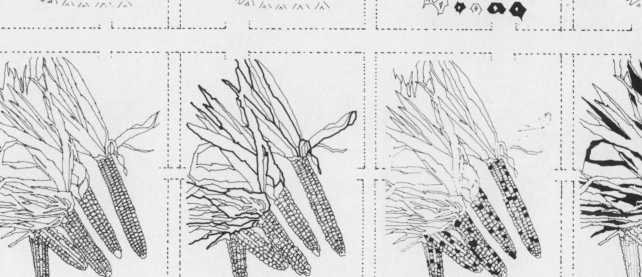

An animal sitting on a branch

1. A simple sketch of the animal is drawn using a few lines only. 2. The tree is shown so as to provide a background to the animal. The light coloured animal is brought out against the textured background. 3. Adding black tone is another way of highlighting the animal against its background. 4. Here, the tree is rendered in dark tone and the animal is kept in white, in order to establish a maximum contrast.

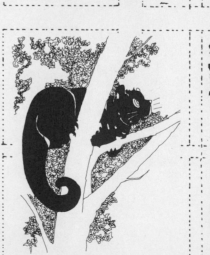

The three examples discussed on the previous page, show a further development of the figures appearing in the last step on page 8.

On this page, three more examples are taken, to show that the approach can be applied to practically any type of sketch. The choice of a particular technique in this approach depends on the nature of the subject matter.

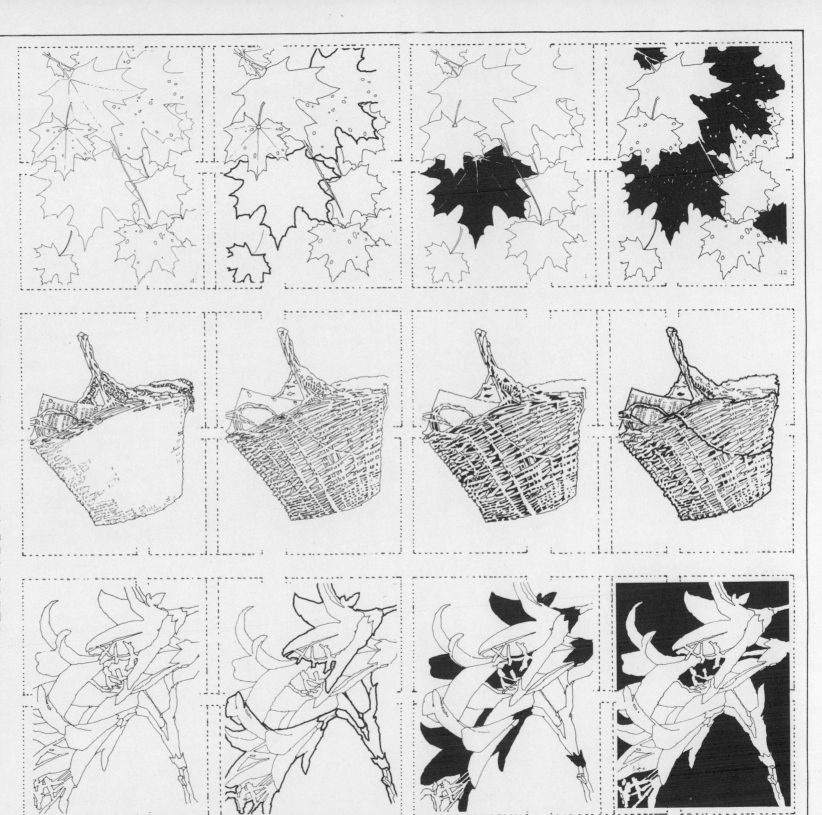

The Maple leaves

1. As shown in the first sketch, the use of fine and uniform *linework* is appropriate, if the sketch does not require a special emphasis. 2. Only some of the leaves are accentuated by drawing their profiles with a heavier line. 3. Only one leaf is brought out in prominence by filling it with a dark tone. It creates a strong focus in the sketch. 4. Adding a dark tone to a number of selected leaves gives a dynamic composition to the sketch.

The wicker basket

1. The contents of the basket are brought into focus by eliminating the constructional details of the remaining part of the basket. 2. A good balance is achieved in the sketch, by showing the construction of the wicker with a delicate *linework*. 3. The construction of the basket is more comprehensible as a result of showing the shadow areas in the weave. 4. The visual strength of the sketch is ascertained by using a thicker line to draw the profile of its various elements. The fine details on the contents add richness to the sketch.

The Lily flowers

1. The delicacy of the flowers is expressed by drawing them with a fine and uniform *linework*. 2. An interesting contrast, between the flowers, is created by showing the profile of the selected flowers with a heavy line. 3. An emphatic contrast is created by adding dark tone to the flowers in the background. 4. The light coloured flowers are highlighted by providing them with the background of a solid tone.

WORKING WITH ILLUSION OF DISTANCE

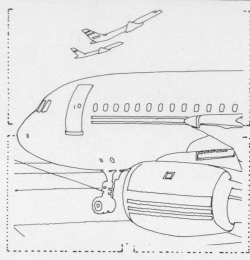

On a two-dimensional surface, as that of a paper, a sketch can be drawn to give a three-dimensional appearance to it. The examples showing the illusion of distance, within the sketch, are dealt with in this section.

● Germ of the idea

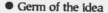

Drawing a small square inside the bigger one and joining their corner points, result into a picture of A DEEP TUNNEL. The effect of the distance is further reinforced by drawing parallel lines with decreasing distance between them, as they approach the centre.

↓

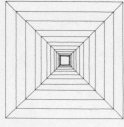

An opposite effect is created when such parallel lines are drawn with increasing distance in between them, as they approach the centre. The result is a picture of A SOLID CONE with a square top, as seen from above.

↓

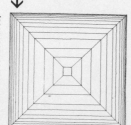

↑
The sketch shows THE STREETSCAPE of the old city hall on Bay street in Toronto. By showing the width of the street with the painted lettering on it - smaller at a distance than at a closer range - an illusion of distance on a horizontal plane is created.

The phenomenon of converging parallel lines, on a vertical plane, is shown in the adjoining example. The vertical elements of A HIGH RISE APARTMENT BUILDING, when looked towards its top, appear to be converging to meet at one point.

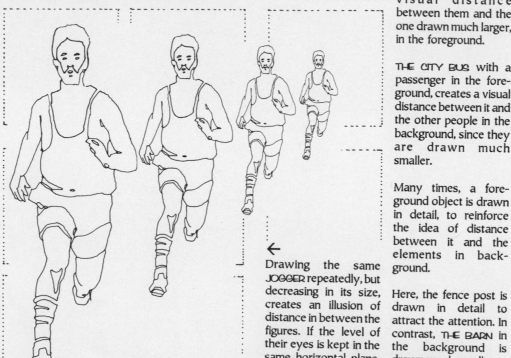

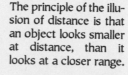

←
Drawing the same JOGGER repeatedly, but decreasing in its size, creates an illusion of distance in between the figures. If the level of their eyes is kept in the same horizontal plane, they would appear to have the same height.

The principle of the illusion of distance is that an object looks smaller at distance, than it looks at a closer range.

THE AIRPLANES. drawn in small size in the background, create a visual distance between them and the one drawn much larger, in the foreground.

THE CITY BUS with a passenger in the foreground, creates a visual distance between it and the other people in the background, since they are drawn much smaller.

Many times, a foreground object is drawn in detail, to reinforce the idea of distance between it and the elements in background.

Here, the fence post is drawn in detail to attract the attention. In contrast, THE BARN in the background is drawn much smaller to convey the idea of its distance from the post.

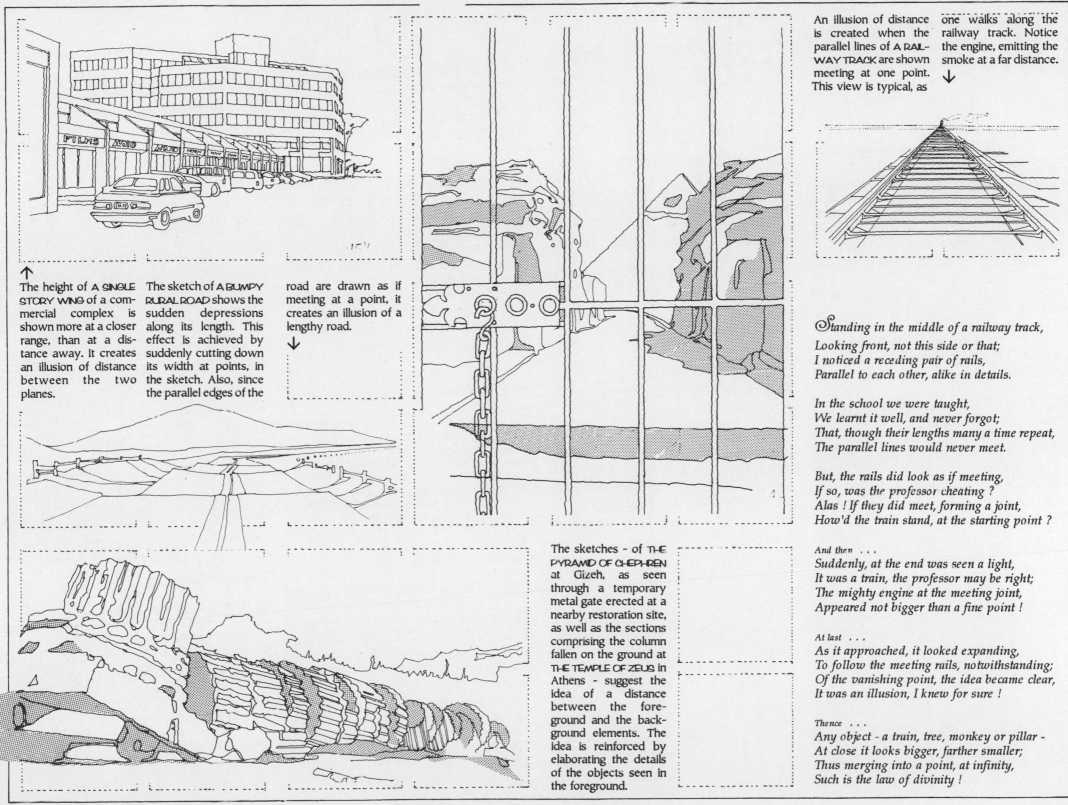

An illusion of distance is created when the parallel lines of A RAIL-WAY TRACK are shown meeting at one point. This view is typical, as one walks along the railway track. Notice the engine, emitting the smoke at a far distance.
↓

↑
The height of A SINGLE STORY WING of a commercial complex is shown more at a closer range, than at a distance away. It creates an illusion of distance between the two planes.

The sketch of A BUMPY RURAL ROAD shows the sudden depressions along its length. This effect is achieved by suddenly cutting down its width at points, in the sketch. Also, since the parallel edges of the road are drawn as if meeting at a point, it creates an illusion of a lengthy road.
↓

The sketches - of THE PYRAMID OF CHEPHREN at Gizeh, as seen through a temporary metal gate erected at a nearby restoration site, as well as the sections comprising the column fallen on the ground at THE TEMPLE OF ZEUS in Athens - suggest the idea of a distance between the foreground and the background elements. The idea is reinforced by elaborating the details of the objects seen in the foreground.

Standing in the middle of a railway track,
Looking front, not this side or that;
I noticed a receding pair of rails,
Parallel to each other, alike in details.

In the school we were taught,
We learnt it well, and never forgot;
That, though their lengths many a time repeat,
The parallel lines would never meet.

But, the rails did look as if meeting,
If so, was the professor cheating ?
Alas ! If they did meet, forming a joint,
How'd the train stand, at the starting point ?

And then ...
Suddenly, at the end was seen a light,
It was a train, the professor may be right;
The mighty engine at the meeting joint,
Appeared not bigger than a fine point !

At last ...
As it approached, it looked expanding,
To follow the meeting rails, notwithstanding;
Of the vanishing point, the idea became clear,
It was an illusion, I knew for sure !

Thence ...
Any object - a train, tree, monkey or pillar -
At close it looks bigger, farther smaller;
Thus merging into a point, at infinity,
Such is the law of divinity !

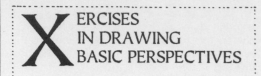

A solid cube is taken as an example to illustrate how to draw a perspective sketch of a simple three-dimensional object. A quick observation of the cube reveals that it has three sets of parallel lines. Each set has four parallel lines, and each of these lines represents an edge of the cube. Each set is perpendicular to the other two sets. The cube has six faces and eight vertex points.

Initially, a three-dimensional sketch of a cube may be drawn as follows :

In this method of projection, a cube is represented by a drawing in which the horizontal edges are drawn at 30 degrees to the base plane. The vertical edges are drawn perpendicular to the horizontal base, all edges being drawn to scale. This method is known as *Isometric projection.*

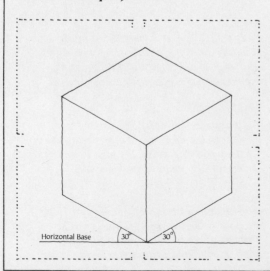

One-point perspective

The parallel lines, receding away from the viewer, appear as if they would meet at one point, when extended. The meeting point, which lies at an infinite distance from the viewer, is called a *Vanishing point.* Since the horizon represents an infinite distance from the viewer, it is considered that the *Vanishing point* lies at the horizon. A horizontal line passing through the *Vanishing point* is thus called the *Line of horizon* or the *Eye level.* It is interesting to learn that, the *Vanishing point,* located at the horizon, represents the position of the viewer's eye, in the sketch. This principle was illustrated earlier in the sketch of a railway track on page 80.

Exercise

To draw a one-point perspective of a given cube :

Let us assume that, a solid cube is placed in front of you and that you intend to draw its one-point perspective. In this position, the front face of the cube is clearly visible to you.

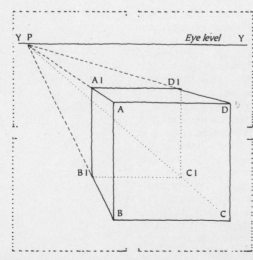

In the following diagram it is assumed that, the square ABCD is the front face of the cube, drawn to scale. YY is the *Eye level* of the viewer. P is the *Vanishing point* on the *Eye level.*

The meaning of the assumed conditions is as follows :

First, the *Vanishing point* indicates the position of the viewers eye and, since in this example it is assumed to be on the left side of the cube, it follows that the viewer is standing on the left side of the cube. Thus, the viewer would see the left face of the cube, also.

Secondly, since the *Eye level* is above the cube, the viewer would see the top face of the cube, as well.

Thus, the viewer is able to see three of the total six faces of the cube.

Join the points A,B,C and D to the *Vanishing point* P. The lines AP, BP, CP, and DP represent a set of parallel lines, extended sufficiently to meet at the *Line of horizon.* Four of the horizontal edges of the cube fall on these lines. Let us assume that BBI represents the length equal to a side of the cube. Draw BIAI parallel to BA, and AIDI parallel to AD. Also, draw in dotted lines, BICI and CIDI parallel to BC and CD respectively. The dotted lines help visualize the remaining three sides of the cube, not visible to the viewer.

Let us now move the position of the viewer, from the left side of the cube to straight ahead in front it, keeping the *Eye level* same as before. Again, the position of the viewer's eye on the *Line of horizon,* is shown by the point P. By vanishing the set of horizontal lines to the point P, and by taking an appropriate measurement for BBI, as before, a new sketch is obtained. Now, only the two faces - the front and the top - of the total six, are visible to the viewer.

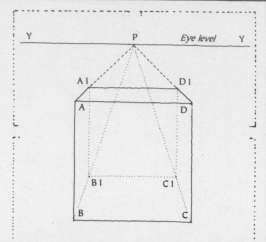

If the viewer now moves to the right side of the cube, the resultant sketch would be as shown.

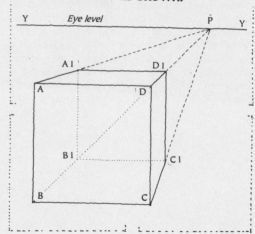

Thus we complete the exercise of drawing a *One-point perspective* of the given cube.

However, in reality, a cube does not appear as drawn is in the three sketches above. In the preceding sketches, the front face of the cube was drawn as a true square. In the first of these three examples, the position of the viewer is assumed to be on the left side of the cube. Thus, the edge AB is closer to him than the edge CD is. According to the rules of perspective, the edge AB would appear larger than the edge CD, and consequently, the lines AD and BC would appear receding away from the viewer. The horizontal lines AD and BC, parallel to each other, also would meet at a point - the second *Vanishing point* - when they are extended.

The line connecting the two *Vanishing points*, is always horizontal and is called the *Line of horizon* or the *Eye level*. While drawing a perspective, the viewer's eye is at this level in relation to the object.

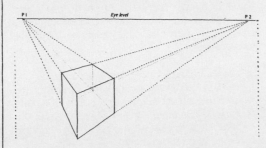

● **To draw a two-point perspective of a given cube :**

Exercise

Let us assume that - AB is the vertical side of the cube, closest to the viewer. YY is the viewer's *Eye level* in relation to the cube to be drawn. And, P1 and P2 are the two *Vanishing points*.

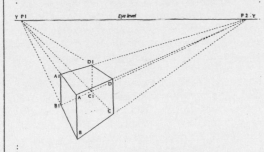

Join the points A & B to the *Vanishing points* P1 and P2. Take point C on the line BP2 in a manner that, when CD is drawn parallel to AB, the area ABCD looks square along the vanishing plane ABP2. Similarly, take point B1 on the line BP1 to form the square ABB1A1 along the vanishing plane ABP1.

The actual length of BB1 is taken smaller than the length BC, since the *Vanishing point* P1 is closer to the central axis AB than the *Vanishing point* P2. Note that, as one *of the Vanishing points* approaches the central axis, the other recedes away from it.

Join A1P2 and DP1, to intersect at D1. Now, the plane ADD1A1 forms the top face of the cube. In the sketch thus completed, three faces of the cube are visible.

The remaining three faces are not visible to the viewer. They could be constructed simply by drawing the lines B1P2 and CP1, to intersect at the point C1, and drawing C1D1. The planes BCC1B1, A1B1C1D1 and CDD1C1 represent the three faces that are not visible.

This sums up the basic principle behind drawing a perspective sketch of a cube, in its three-dimensional form, as we see it in reality.

● **Taking measurements along the horizontal and vertical axes :**

Exercise

For this exercise, assume that BC is one unit in length. Here, the exercise is to plot the unit measurements along the line BP2, in the direction of the *Vanishing point* P2.

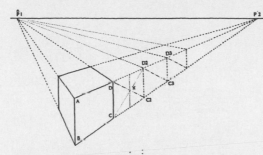

Draw a line DC2, parallel to AC. CC2 is the unit length, equal to BC, measured along the vanishing plane. Draw C2D2 parallel to AB cutting AP2 at D2. Repeat the same procedure, by drawing D2C3 parallel to DC2, C3D3 parallel to AB . . . and so on, to obtain a range of unit length measurements along the line BP2.

For a fractional module, say a half, join CD2 intersecting DC2 at X. Through X, draw a line parallel to AB, cutting CC2 and DD2, into two equal parts. Use the same procedure to obtain the unit measurements as well as the fractions along the line BP1.

It is now easy to draw more than one cube, placed side by side, in the direction of points P1 and P2.

For example, if you need to draw a pair of cubes placed side by side, in the direction of P2, the overall length of the pair would be two units, indicated by the line BC2.

In this case, the front face of the pair would be shown by ABC2D2. D2 is then joined to P1, to intersect A1P2 at E. Thus, the top face of the pair would be shown by AD2EA1.

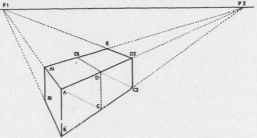

However, for taking the vertical measurements, simply use the side AB as a scale.

For example, if the height of the solid mass is 1.5 units, then take BW equal to 1.5 times AB. Join WP1 and WP2. Extend CD and B1A1 to meet these lines at X and Z, respectively. Join XP1 and ZP2 to intersect at Y. The three faces of the extended solid figure are BCXW, BB1ZW and WXYZ.

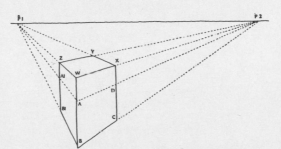

The principle explained above, also holds good for drawing more complex objects.

Of the basic solids, having straight edges,
The cube is studied, to construct images;
The principle, once thoroughly understood,
For all other objects, it holds good.

The method includes, the vanishing points,
For two sets of parallel lines;
The professor taught us how to plot,
For any situation, thanks a lot !

The object may be big or small,
Simple, complex, flat or tall;
As, a box, a house or a shopping mall,
A matter of practice, that's all !

Hence . . .
Just studying a cube alone,
The properties of all, are known;
Simply discovering how to measure,
Pythagoras enjoyed Trigonometry's pleasure !

YET, ANOTHER APPLICATION

An art of creating a finished architectural perspective is a complex one. It requires the knowledge of constructing a perspective, usually in pencil, of any type of building. An ample material is available on this subject alone, and therefore, no special effort has been made to explain it in the present chapter.

The view of a building as seen from its outside, is called an *Exterior perspective*. Similarly, a view of any of its inside is termed as an *Interior perspective*.

Having constructed the perspective of a building in pencil, one needs to add other information to it, such as, people, trees, signs and other appropriate elements. These elements have to be drawn in the sketch at suitable places, so as to enhance the composition of the overall sketch.

An application of freehand *linework* in ink, to the perspectives already completed in pencil, is discussed in this section.

● The sequence

The sketch shows an exterior view of a multistoried building on a busy intersection. Notice the composition. Main building, the centre of interest, is flanked by the trees on both the sides. A limited but suggestive *linework* on the main building, the delicate *linework* on the historical building on the left as well as on the massive tree on the right, add a touch of fineness to the composition.

Step 1

Contemplate on the sketch, regarding its overall size, and assess the proper thickness of *linework* required to draw it. The idea is to choose the right thickness of the nib so that the sketch, when completed, would not look too heavy or too weak.

Step 2

Start inking the elements of the foreground first. By this way, you need not draw the part of the background that is superimposed by the foreground elements. According to the rules of perspective, elements in the foreground appear larger than those of the same size, but at a distance away. Therefore, in many cases, the elements in the foreground tend to cover a substantial part of the elements in the background.

In the adjoining sketch, the large tree on the right-hand side in the foreground as well as the smaller tree on the left, cover a part of the main building behind them. By drawing the trees in the foreground first, the covered part of the building is not required to be drawn.

However, if the background elements are drawn prior to drawing the foreground elements, the *linework* would get intermixed and become messy.

Step 3

While drawing the elements in the foreground, a decision has to be made as to how much of the background they should cover.

Referring to the above sketch again, notice that the historic building and the tree on the left, cover up to more than half of the corner of the main building. The profile of the tree on the right is drawn so as to leave the upper part of the rear section, clearly visible through the foliage.

Following this line of thought, one may conclude that - the elements that cover the ones behind them, are to be drawn first, to avoid superimposition of *linework*. This process completes the foreground scenario.

Step 4

To draw a building, first take note of the continuity of certain elements, such as, the columns, the beams, the spandrel etc. Many buildings display a repetitive pattern of windows. In order to break such monotony, some of the windows may be drawn only partially, to form a well-balanced composition. Care must be taken that the essence is conveyed properly.

Notice the handling of a repetitive pattern in the above example. Each line, horizontal or vertical, is drawn fully, before starting the next one.

Step 5

After completion of the sketch to this extent, it should be seen with squinted eyes, to check its balance in terms of the line mass, texture, etc. It may be necessary to add extra *linework* to emphasise certain area or to explain certain detail.

In order to add texture and to ensure a proper balance, the railing and the other details on the right side are added to the sketch.

This completes the proper sequence required to draw a perspective sketch of a building in simple *linework*. The steps explained above are applicable, in principle, to all types of exterior or interior sketches of the buildings.

On-site study of Buland Darvaza, Fatehpur Sikri, India.

A museum building, a proposal.

↑
Eglinton Mills, Toronto

The sketch of this proposed seven storied building shows treatment of the repetitive elements of its facade. The use of *Ziptone* is appropriate here to show the shadows of the building blocks.

The sketch of the low-rise building shows the use of a fine *linework*, the texture and *Ziptone*. Here, *Ziptone* is used to indicate glass. The interior space is clearly visible through the glass surface, against the brightness of the exterior.
↓

An office building interior

The interior perspective of a three storied high lobby shows a combination of *linework* and *Ziptone* creating a soft contrast.

On-site study of Parthenon on the Acropolis, Athens.

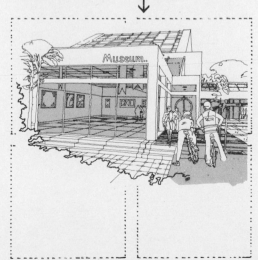

Through the ages, the need for a shelter,
Even the sages did not alter;
To sketch a shelter, no need to falter,
Once perfected, no room for helter-skelter.

Of the 3-D objects, having straight edges,
Buildings form the fascinating subjects;
The principle of drawing, is easy too,
As explained on the pages, 81 and 82.

Delineating a building, full or in part,
Compare it not, with an aimless dart;
Truest of all hearts - yes, a mother's heart,
Architecture is the mother of all arts !

ZIPTONE FOR SOFT CONTRAST

Grey tones of various shades are available in art shops under the trade name of *Ziptone*. It is used for adding a soft contrast, to add a desired depth to the sketch.

Ziptone is easy to cut with a pen-knife. Being peel-and-stick type, it can be applied conveniently to the sketch.

← A simple patch of grey tone gives strength to the sketch of THE STUDENT testing his skill on a drawing pad.

→ Also, in the sketch of THE MAN READING A NEWSPAPER, the same idea is employed. Notice the fineness of the dot size of the grey tone in relation to the *linework*, in each case.

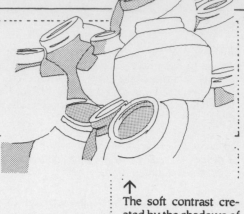

↑ The soft contrast created by the shadows of THE CLAY POTS, results into an interesting graphic effect.

→ The profile of the land mass is brought out by creating a subtle contrast between the grey and the white areas in the sketch of THE GLOBE.

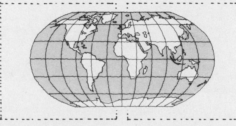

Taking a sketch of THE ZINNIA FLOWERS as an example, a comparative study of various shades of *Ziptone*, is made in a set of the following six drawings.

The first drawing shows the basic sketch of the zinnia flowers.

The second drawing shows the use of a very light *grade of Ziptone*. The contrast introduced by it is barely noticeable, but is enough to inject a softness to the sketch.

The third drawing shows the use of a light grade of *Ziptone*. It introduces a subtle contrast and it takes away the flatness present in the first sketch.

The fourth drawing displays the use of a medium grade of *Ziptone*. It gives a balanced contrast between the lit and the shaded areas.

The fifth drawing employs a heavier grade of *Ziptone*. In this sketch a hard contrast between the lit and the shaded areas, is evident.

Here, a solid tone is used to depict the shadow pattern. The intensity of the shade has reached its limit of darkness to a maximum. It makes the sketch appear unnatural.

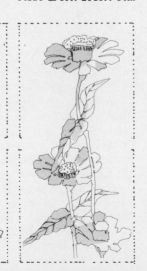  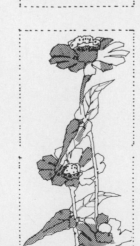 

In the adjoining sketch of THE CHINESE VASE, *Ziptone* is applied in patches, sporadically distributed, to emphasize the decorative motif and to suggest the shadow pattern on it.

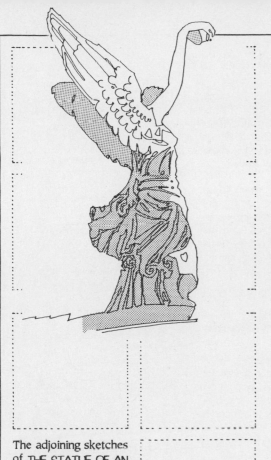

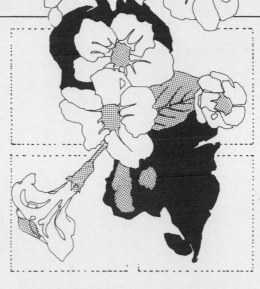

↑ Choosing the proper area for *Ziptone* helps identify the profiles in the sketch of THE BABY AND THE GIRL

The profile of THE WOMAN in the front, is brought out by using *Ziptone* on the chosen areas of the sketch. ↓

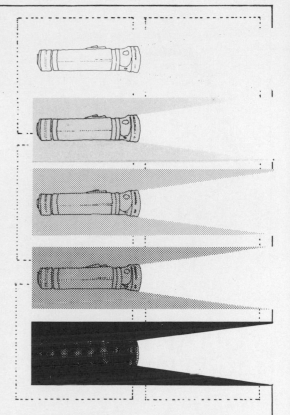

The IPOMOEA FLOWERS show the use of a solid tone along with the *Ziptone*. Here, the background of a black tone enhances the whiteness of the white. The proximity of black adds sharpness to the grey tone. While, the black and grey tones near the white tone impart a stepped-up contrast to the elements. Solid tone also helps add an interest to the sketch and ties the sketch together.

The adjoining sketches of THE STATUE OF AN ANGEL and THE POP CANS. show the shadow patterns on them. The use of grey tone helps indicate the direction of the sunlight.

← The delicate nature of THE POPPY FLOWERS is realistically depicted with the use of a combination of very fine *linework* and the grey tone.

→ A light grey *Ziptone* is appropriately used to bring out the delicacy of THE WATER LILIES.

While in slumber, a torch once thought,
If the sun lights earth, why can I not ?

At noon time, it opened its eye,
Hardly to compare, with a firefly.

Losing no patience, it pushed on,
Until the twilight noticed, it was on.

Then came the eve, when the sun grew weak,
The torch kept on, but not at its peak.

Start of the night, sun gave up the fight,
The little torch knew, he could be right.

The middle of the night, in the blinding dark,
The torch now made, the brightest mark !

Throughout the time, Ziptone was the witness,
Helped the little torch, attain brightness !

CHAPTER EIGHT

Summary of techniques
... changing the moods

The application of various ideas discussed in the previous chapter is illustrated here, by taking a single example of A GIRL PLAYING MUSIC, from page 24. The same example is used to illustrate a number of techniques, so that a comparative study of their results can be done properly.

The suitability of a particular technique, or a combination of the techniques, depends upon the intended impact for the sketch.

● **Aiming for the least**
→

The technique of drawing the sketch with a minimum number of lines is illustrated here. Notice the simplicity of the sketch. The sketch has retained the essence, without being burdened by too many details.

● **Connections at nodes**
← →

The technique of *Cross connections* and *Altering the flow of lines* is illustrated in the adjoining two examples.

Notice the rough appearance of the first sketch. The continuity of the lines and the resulting softness in the second sketch, are evident.

● **Emphasizing with heavy lines**
←

The use of heavy lines has imparted a prominence to the figure in the foreground, as compared to its background.

→

In the second sketch, the background is emphasized with heavy lines and the figure plays a secondary role.

● **Flow of heavy lines**
→

A meandering heavy line through the sketch creates a play between thick and thin lines, and adds a new dimension to it.

● **Importance of texture**
←

The concentration of texture transfers the centre of attention to the hair.

→

The separation of the areas of texture divides the focus of attention. The area chosen for applying texture depends on the intended result.

→

An introduction of a solid tone adds a punch to the sketch. It produces a stronger contrast than the texture obtained by *linework*. The solid black tone of in background highlights the delicate texture of the fine *linework*.

● Key to compositions

←

A rectangular composition is achieved by filling the entire frame in the background, with the pattern. Notice that, as a result of using a single thickness of line for the whole sketch, the figure and the background blend with each other well.

→

By showing the pattern in the background in part only, a diagonal composition is achieved.

● On focus of Interest

→

The figure is brought into prominence by creating a high contrasting background. An introduction of a geometric grid, as a backdrop, sets up a good contrast between the rigid lines of the pattern, and the free flowing *linework* of the figure itself.

● Random distribution of solid tones

←

In this case, only some parts of the figure are highlighted by filling them with a solid tone. The elements to be highlighted are selected so as to maintain the balance of the sketch. It causes a movement of the eye from one part of the sketch to the other.

→

By adding a suitable background and reselecting the areas to be toned, an abstract composition is achieved. The random distribution of the accentuated elements dominates the remaining weaker *linework*.

● Setting up the contrast

→

A light and shadow effect is created by the contrasting solid tone. The moonlight falling on the girl highlights certain parts of her body, while the dark tones portray the shadow areas.

→

By filling the entire figure with a solid tone, a silhouette effect is created. In this case, the girl appears to be standing inside the room against the bright sky in the background.

● Illusion of distance

→

By introducing a smaller figure, against its own dark background, an illusion is created as if another musician at a distance is visible through a window.

● Ziptone

→

By choosing a proper grade of *Ziptone*, the sketch is given a softer contrast.

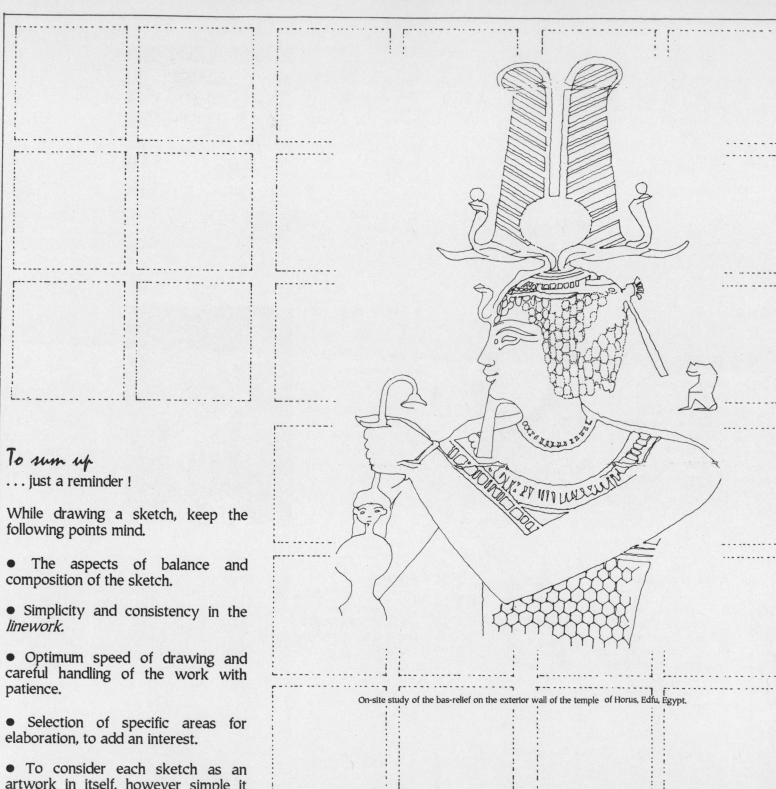

On-site study of the bas-relief on the exterior wall of the temple of Horus, Edfu, Egypt.

To sum up

... just a reminder !

While drawing a sketch, keep the following points mind.

- The aspects of balance and composition of the sketch.

- Simplicity and consistency in the *linework*.

- Optimum speed of drawing and careful handling of the work with patience.

- Selection of specific areas for elaboration, to add an interest.

- To consider each sketch as an artwork in itself, however simple it may be.

Modern age of technology and science,
Ruled by polished tools - the man's reliance;
Caused dependency, confusion and a crisis,
Losing, I fear, the good old learning basis.

And besides ...
To burden with gadgets, devoid of passion,
Before learning simplicity - the basic lesson;
Is like, using the head, not the heart,
Or, putting the horse behind the cart !

And ...
The advancement of man, is, but less,
If depending on gadgets, is called progress;
As toys they are fine, for fun and wonder,
Good for convenience, not to surrender.

Technology gave us, the modern boon,
And with it, a passport to the moon;
But, of course, tagged with a condition,
Not suitable for human habitation.

For example ...
The beauty of moon, is only from a distance,
Expressed in poetry, since human existence;
Where water flows not, and birds don't sing,
That is, simple joys, which does not bring;
Is good for a trip, for a scientist or a king,
Not as an abode, for a human being.

Therefore ...
Is it really wise, to settle on the satellite,
Thinking it a novelty;
And depend on a thermos-flask,
To enjoy a simple cup of tea ?

Or put it this way ...
Living on the moon, may be a possible task,
But, your life depends on the Oxygen mask;
Without such gizmo, on earth you can bask,
To breathe fresh air, no need to ask !

Thus ...
Many find the true beauty,
In the revival of simplicity;
Like - enjoy building castles in sand,
Or, receiving pat with a loving hand !

Therefore, ...
Those right down to earth,
Wanting to enjoy, pleasure of art, and mirth;
May find beauty in the lines fresh, and,
Drawn with a touch of human hand !

Soon, the ball starts rolling automatically. Once the mind is given a chance to concentrate, with a positive attitude, it automatically takes delight in discovering the potential of creativity further and further.

The earlier you put your heart in practising the freehand *linework*, the more fun you will have. You will reap the joy, starting it at any age. Once developed, it would be a part of you and would prove to be one of the greatest gifts you will have presented to yourself !

Before the farewell was finally bade,
In the end my teachers said :
"By reading you will gain, page by page,
But only the second-hand knowledge.

"Reading is good, it has an advantage,
If the aim be, a theoretical privilege;
But, - practice gives man the insight -
Who would deny the importance of it ?

Because ...
"A single deed excels a hundred word,
A simple start surpasses plans absurd;
At any age, any stage, starting once,
Helps one gain - the initial experience.

And, therefore, ...
"With continued practice, the experience,
And, consequently, the pragmatic cognizance;
Irreplaceable it is, on which you may count,
For that special touch, without a doubt !"

In closing
. . . it is really easy !

The important step, in getting conversant with the art of sketching with freehand lines, is to *get started*. A handy tool, such as a pencil or a pen is all you need. A habit of drawing quick little sketches, however primary it may sound, builds up a foundation for the treasure of fun to follow. No sophisticated tools, special equipment or an arduous practice is really necessary. Initially, you may not succeed in getting good results, but a little patience will provide you with the necessary confidence.

We are, or become, those things which we repeatedly do. Therefore, excellence can become not just an event but a habit.

. . . Albert Einstein

Index
... for convenience

● The author is grateful to the following individuals for their enthusiastic participation in putting this work in the present form.

Typesetting and
General assistance :
Dr. Ratnakar Narale

Assistance in Layout :
Mr. Attileo Labriola